Voices
from the
Streets

Young Former Gang Members Tell Their Stories

Interviews and Photographs by **S. Beth Atkin**

Little, Brown and Company
BOSTON NEW YORK TORONTO LONDON

Also by S. Beth Atkin
Voices from the Fields:
Children of Migrant Farmworkers Tell Their Stories

First Edition

Excerpt from "Feel No Pain," by Helen Adu, Stuart Matthewman, and Andrew Hale, copyright © 1992 Sony Music Publishing UK Ltd./Angel Music Ltd. By permission of Sony Music Publishing, 8 Music Square, Nashville, TN 37203.

Spanish translation of "My Name" by Enrique Degregori and Amy Pofcher.

"Hope Is a Diamond," by Valerie Tyson, copyright © by Valerie Tyson.
Reprinted by permission of the author.

Student quotations in "Hope" section from "How to Survive Urban Violence with Hope,"
by Evelyn McLean Brady, *English Journal*, September 1995. Copyright © 1995
by the National Council of Teachers of English.
By permission of the National Council of Teachers of English.

Library of Congress Cataloging-in-Publication Data

Voices from the streets : young former gang members tell their stories /
interviews and photographs by S. Beth Atkin.
  p. cm.
  Summary: Photographs, poems, and interviews with former gang members from different regions of the United States depict their experiences.
  ISBN 0-316-05634-0
  1. Gangs—United States—Case studies—Juvenile literature. 2. Gang members—United States—Interviews—Juvenile literature. 3. Youth—United States—Attitudes—Juvenile literature. [1. Gangs. 2. Gang members—Interviews.] I. Atkin, S. Beth.
  HV6439.U5V65 1996
  364.1′06′0973—dc20   95-26757
       10 9 8 7 6 5 4 3 2 1

Q-KP

Published simultaneously in Canada by Little, Brown & Company (Canada) Limited

Printed in the United States of America

For my family
And in memory of Frank Rosas,
who had hope, wanted to improve his life,
and did

Contents

Foreword

Not too long ago, a thirteen-year-old boy—I'll call him Antoine—visited my home. Antoine lives in the Rockwell Gardens public housing complex on Chicago's west side. I had met him while reporting a story on public housing, and I hadn't seen him in three or four years. It was an unusually hot spring day when he stopped by, so I lent Antoine, who was wearing a nylon jogging suit, a pair of shorts, which he reluctantly slipped on. They exposed a tattoo just above his ankle: a five-pointed star, the symbol for one of Chicago's street gangs. I made him put his sweatpants back on—and let him know how disappointed I was. I could have done more. I should have. But what made me think that even more is what I later learned from one of Antoine's friends. Antoine's mother, it turns out, wasn't around much. He apparently hoped this tattoo would win her attention or draw her ire. It did neither. She saw the tattoo—and barely commented on it. That just cemented Antoine's allegiance to the gang.

As I read the startling candid tales of the former gang members in this book, it is clear to me where the answers lie: with the adults, whether they be parents, ministers, community outreach workers, neighbors, even police or teachers. Almost all the young men and women interviewed in these pages point to some adult who nurtured them, guided them, and provided some sense of future. Says twenty-year-old Haywood Rogers of a neighborhood minister: "He gives me a lot of hope. . . . Even if I choose the wrong side, I know he's still there. And I can humble myself and say I made a mistake." I'm reminded of graffiti covering a piece of plywood nailed across an abandoned storefront on Chicago's west side. I would pass it on the way to work each morning. In red magic marker, a child had scrawled: "I like myself. I like myself. I like myself. I like myself." Children cry out for affirmation from the adult world.

Beth Atkin's interviews reveal the silence in many children's lives: both institutional and self-imposed. The schools, police, public housing authorities, the juvenile courts, sometimes the family—all there presumably to help serve children—often are mute in the company of troubled youth. As I listen to the reflections of these former gang members, I'm struck how rare is the forceful, constructive, and loving intervention of these institutions. One boy tells of a social worker who told his mother that he "wasn't gonna amount to nothing." Two other children tell of being expelled from school. One girl talks of being mistreated by the police. And many talk about neglectful parents. "Listen to [kids]," suggests thirteen-year-old Elena Rojas, "'cause kids like to be listened to." Such simple yet sage advice.

Faced with a suffocating sense of aloneness, the children remain silent themselves as well. Part of it is, undoubtedly, out of a feeling of shame or embarrassment. But much of it is, I'm sure, out of a fear that if they were to share all that they've heard and seen, they might not be believed or, perhaps just as worse, would have their experiences dismissed. So often I hear that the children get used to the violence. Nonsense. How could anyone become accustomed to losing friends or relatives? Saroeum Phoung, a Cambodian immigrant interviewed in these pages, talks about his family running from the brutal Khmer Rouge. "My parents would not talk about what happened in Cambodia," he says. "They just keep it to themselves. That's why they get crazy." Much the same could be said of the children from our central cities.

Beth Atkin has given a voice to some of these children. And with frankness, self-awareness, and poignancy, the young men and women we meet remind us that for all their anger and bravado as gang members, they were, indeed, just children. Searching. Questioning. Needy. And playful. Like Antoine, they want and need an adult to pay attention. They want and need adults to help break the silence.

Alex Kotlowitz

Introduction

I became interested in gangs while researching my last book, *Voices from the Fields*, about the children of migrant farmworkers. Many of the teachers, counselors, police officers, and families I consulted in connection with that book were profoundly concerned about how dangerous and widespread gangs were in their communities. So for one chapter, I interviewed Frank Rosas, a seventeen-year-old boy who had been in a gang in Soledad, California, a small town populated mostly by Latino farmworkers.

Meeting Frank challenged my preconceptions about gang members. He was well spoken, polite, intelligent, and ambitious. He was not happy with his gang involvement, which he had chosen to protect himself, and saw that it had begun to ruin his chance for a good education and future. Frank finally did find a way out. When he left the gang, he also had to leave his school to avoid retribution by rival gang members. He began studying for his GED and working full-time. On one occasion, he left his work in the fields, drove forty miles home to shower and change, then returned to help me greet customers at a book signing. I remember thinking then, Who would believe that this is a former *gang* member?

Interviewing and photographing Frank Rosas motivated me to work with other gang members who were trying to leave their gangs and improve their lives. A poem by Leticia Orozco, "Hey Ése: To all the gangs," which accompanies Frank's chapter in *Voices from the Fields*, captures what I wanted to reveal about Frank and other gang members like him:

> *You, with your sincere and sweet soul,*
> *you, who carries a child crying inside of you*
> *and needs to be calmed . . .*
>
> *I didn't know the simplicity that exists in your heart*
>
> *I have found that I now admire you. . . .*
> *You mean danger to me,*
> *but also you mean sweetness.*

The history of youth gangs in America extends back as far as the late 1700s. However, with the spread of drugs and guns, the character of youth gangs is vastly different from what it was even twenty years ago. Between 1980 and 1993, gang-related murders of and by juveniles have increased fourfold. And although some of the reasons for joining, such as discrimination and unemployment, have remained the same, many new and disturbing reasons have also arisen. I wanted, in the portraits that make up this book, to touch upon the major reasons kids now join gangs: violent neighborhoods, family breakdown, racism, poverty, and poor access to education and decent-paying jobs.

Most important, I wanted my book to carry a positive message, to bring hope. This would mean showing not only why kids join gangs but also how they are able to leave them. For this reason, I chose to interview and photograph former gang members—teenagers and young adults no longer involved. The reality of their lives would give the most insightful information, some answers if not solutions, and the greatest optimism.

As the kids in this book will tell you, there are no easy ways out of gang life; it takes courage, time, dedication, hard work, a strong desire to change, and acceptance that no one else can do it for you. It also takes support from intervention programs, teachers, counselors, and others, including former gang members, who are often the most effective in reaching at-risk youth. Some former gang youths are now employed at the programs that helped them get out of gangs, demonstrating these programs' value. The two adults interviewed in this book bring the important perspective of the many conscientious people who are doing this difficult but rewarding work. Like the youths in this book, they provide a positive but realistic point of view.

I wanted my book not to glamorize gang members but to portray them with respect. I knew that many readers would find it hard to sympathize with kids from gangs. In my last book, the migrant children naturally evoked empathy. They could easily be seen as children with limited choices hoping to improve their lives. But gang members, even the youngest ones, seem to have the choice of whether to join a gang. And it is not easy to look beyond their connections to crimes, violence, and drugs. But after spending months with these children, I saw that they had been faced with more than many people face in a lifetime. They had responsibilities most adults would find tough to deal with. Often what they told me was so disturbing, I had to turn off my tape recorder and take a break. Whether it was about being in Khmer Rouge camps in Cambodia, taken to crack houses as a child, or beaten up by a boyfriend at thirteen, I would forget I was listening to someone so young. I saw adult experiences in their eyes. When I was first taking pictures, smiles were something they seemed to ration. A seriousness, startling for their ages, seemed to always be there. Then I would get a glimpse of just how young they were while they joked with a friend, hugged their mom, danced, or played sports. I had to remind myself to try to capture their specific type of youth: fear and pain as well as joy and vulnerability.

As I was working on this book, people often asked me, "Aren't you scared?" What allayed my fears was seeing how courageous and fearless these kids are. I still find where they came from and what they had to overcome difficult to believe. They helped me see how violence is a normal part of their lives. As one police officer said, guns are as easy to get as Popsicles. As Elena says in chapter 3, "You can get guns given to you for free. They're stolen—they'll just give them to you." The crimes are more random than ever and committed by more children and teens than ever. It is hard to comprehend that more teenagers are killed by firearms than by all natural causes combined. One reason I persisted working on this project is that these former gang members' participation in and response to violence actually made sense to me within the context of their lives. As Hewitt Joyner III says in chapter 9, "When they see someone get shot in front of them at age two, they're going to get used to it. By the time they reach fourteen, just think of the way that kid's going to think." More and more children today are desensitized to violence. Watching siblings, friends, and neighbors get shot is part of their childhood experience, and in that context, shooting a gun becomes a normal response to fear. Surrounded by violence, kids can also turn to guns as a way to fit in and be "cool." Joining a gang is an attempt to fulfill basic human needs—protection, support, and belonging.

Our justice system has responded to the rising violence by sending kids to jail sooner and with longer sentences. Some people reason that jail at least keeps kids off the streets, and some believe that it will change their thinking and behavior. But unfortunately studies have shown that jail has little rehabilitative powers on youths. In fact, it often acts as a training ground, turning kids into tougher criminals and gang members than they were when they entered. Not only do some gang members use their incarceration as a way to earn respect, but prison gangs, often affiliated with street gangs, recruit both from inside and outside prisons. Also, adapting to jail can be the only education these kids receive, for once in jail at a young age, many don't finish school. As more and more studies have proven, longer sentences have little impact on adolescents.

Instead, many believe that the best solution lies with early intervention. Intervention programs work with children as young as six as well as their parents, and use a variety of approaches, including family, group, and individual counseling and activities such as sports, art, and field trips. They can be very effective in heading off behavior that results in kids joining gangs. As this book tries to show, intervention is often these kids' only chance. Programs mentioned in the book are listed in an appendix, along with information on how kids can go about finding help, including access to a nationwide program list.

So how did I find these programs and kids? Through a lot of research and through the help of teachers, counselors, outreach workers, psychologists, lawyers, judges, social workers, doctors, and students. I spent several years traveling and researching to find youths with diverse, compelling, and unusual stories. My goal was to find exemplary programs and teens who were improving their lives and who could be honest with me. Generally they wanted to let their stories be published to help others. Some agreed to participate at the suggestion of a parent, counselor, or mentor as a way to help them resolve their gang involvement.

To break down stereotypes of gang youths, I chose both boys and girls of different ages and ethnicities from a variety of locations. These kids show that gang members today are not always from urban areas, not all African American, that girls can be "real" gang members, and that Latino/Hispanic gang members are not always Puerto Rican or Mexican. They also show that not all gang members want to be in gangs instead of holding jobs and that they are not always uneducated and violent. It is also important to see that not all these kids blame their parents for their need to belong to a gang. Many credit their parents and are proud of them. Others have had difficult family circumstances but are trying to understand their family's struggles and to repair ties and communication.

I have not changed the words of the kids I interviewed, making only minor edits for clarity. I felt that to understand these kids, we need to hear from them in their own voices, incorrect grammar and profanity included. Gang-related words or other terms that might be unfamiliar to the reader are defined in the glossary. The book also features some of the youths' own writing, such as poems and journal entries, along with some of their favorite quotations, to further capture their struggles and dreams. Some writing from kids not interviewed in this book, but from other intervention programs and schools, is also included.

I consciously decided not to take photos that sensationalize gangs. Many gang members disapprove of the image portrayed of them in the media. Although photos of gangs showing their gang hand signs, standing near graffiti, or holding guns are powerful and startling, putting former gang members in their old neighborhoods or with current gang members would be a false portrayal of their present lives and would be dangerous for them as well as manipulative. Some of the photographs in the book show former gang members still within the context of their difficult circumstances—poor neighborhoods, often still surrounded by violence. But even with these images, I tried for a positive tone, consistent with the purpose of this book.

Working with these kids for over two years helped me balance their interviews and photographs between their maturity and their youth and between their strengths and their weaknesses. I tried to be sure that the portraits that emerged were full and unbiased. I was with the kids at school, on the street, at the programs they attended or helped run. I met their teachers, girlfriends, boyfriends, spouses, and children and had dinner at their homes. I was involved in their lives, and I developed good relationships with them and many of their families. I still talk to them about getting jobs, making decisions about going to college, and I call them on their birthdays. When one of them called me long distance at 1:30 A.M. to say his wife was going into labor, I knew I had something other than these youths' honesty and trust; I had their friendship. This is not to say they were not, at times, hard to deal with. But these kids constantly revealed parts of themselves that gave hope and offered proof that even troubled kids from dysfunctional families can have better lives. They also showed me that kids in gangs can be extraordinary people.

Beating the odds has not been simple for them, though, and while these youths are no longer in gangs, their lives are still extremely trying and complicated. And as they struggle, they often wish they could go back to the gang for support. Many of them speak with longing about the gang: "I want a strong future, but sometimes I have that feeling of going back to the street," Saroeum Phoung says in chapter 2. "I almost slipped through the edge and said, 'Damn, let's go back to the gang.' Because it made me feel warm. People don't reject you; they want you." Some were or are still in danger, under indictment, coping with the violent deaths of friends or relatives, dealing with abusive or absent parents, or having to care for their own children. Their lives are hard, but they still find the time to attend, contribute to, or develop and run gang intervention programs. They also gave me a great deal of their time. After all they have been through, they are still willing to try to help themselves and others. Even after being hard-core gang members, some have become heroes and role models in their communities.

As resilient and persevering as these kids are, though, I still worry that I will hear that one has gone back to his or her gang or has been shot. Or that they have lost the ability or desire to improve their lives. I never know what to expect when I speak with them because their lives change constantly. Mostly I worry that with all these changes and hardships, they will give up hope.

Still, I know that believing in them and showing them that their lives can be repaired is a key step to keeping them, and others like them, alive. They have taught me that being in a gang was a way for them to adapt to their neighborhoods, homes, and families in a society that is not just theirs but also mine.

I: WALKING IN
Why Kids Join Gangs

"I thought if my mom found out about the gang, she would take me more seriously. I thought she might pay attention." —*Brandy, age 12*

"You come to this country, people look at you differently. Treat you like dirt. It makes you feel hopeless. So now where do people turn? Like me, I turned to a gang. . . . We were like a family, a government, a rule. Just a system for ourselves." —*Saroeum, age 22*

"I was tired of being picked on. . . . I wanted them to really, really protect me, and I wanted to be feared." —*Elena, age 13*

"I guess if you are around good people, you're more than likely gonna be a good person. If you're around bad people, you're more than likely gonna be a bad person. . . . It depends on who you fall in with." —*Patrick, age 16*

Serenity Prayer

God, grant me the serenity to accept the things I cannot change,
The courage to change the things I can,
And the wisdom to know the difference.

ONE

No One Around

Children and teens often turn to gangs for a sense of family, a sense of support, security, and love, which they feel is lacking in their own homes. Once in a gang, they adopt gang values, just as a child adopts its family's values. They develop a deep trust in and loyalty to their gang.

Dramatic increases in drugs, poverty, and unemployment as well as a growing divorce rate have all contributed to the pervasive breakdown of the American family. While neglect and abuse certainly occur in families with two parents, it can be more prevalent when just one parent carries the responsibility of supporting and raising the children. Over 25 percent of children in the United States are raised by single parents. Figures are higher for Latino/Hispanic children and at least double for African Americans. Early intervention, which includes working with both parent and child, can help restore some stability to families of at-risk kids.

For much of her life, twelve-year-old Brandy Egland was raised in Columbus, Ohio, by her aunt and uncle, and she also spent time living in Florida with her mother. She was involved in gangs in both locations. At the time of our interviews, she was attending a residential rehabilitation program at The Starting Place in Hollywood, Florida, one of the few programs her mother could find that accepted gang-involved twelve-year-olds.

Brandy Egland

When I was little, I remember my mom was always going somewhere to get good drugs. So I lived in different places and went back and forth from Florida to Ohio a lot. I was born in Florida, but my whole family is from Ohio. My dad lived there, but he died from too much alcohol and drugs. I never met him, and I didn't really know about him. My mom doesn't remember anything good about my dad because he was high all the time. She was on drugs, too. And one of her sisters got murdered because of drugs. Even my grandmother smokes weed. My mom put one of my stepbrothers up for adoption because she didn't have enough money to take care of him. All she had money for was her drugs.

I went to live with my aunt and uncle near Columbus when I was five. They are the ones who really raised me. Then my mom came to Ohio from Florida when I was six. I moved in with her there, but then we went to Pennsylvania to live with her parents so she could use her money for drugs. When I was seven, we went to Arizona.

I was a very, very destructive child. Once, in Arizona, my baby-sitter called Children's Services 'cause I tore her whole entire house up. I took the scissors

Brandy with her mother

and went over her bed until she would give me a cigarette. My mom didn't come home for four days to get me—she was out getting high. And the sitter got sick and tired of me. So I was in a foster home for a while. Then we went back to Florida. After, I went back up to Ohio to live with my aunt Christine and my uncle and two cousins again.

I missed out on my childhood because of my mom. I lost twelve years. I thought I was responsible for her. Like all those times, when kids were playing Barbie dolls, I had to call my grandfather to go pick her up from the crack house. She used to smoke crack in front of me. But I didn't know what it was then. She took me to crack houses. They stink. There's no food in them, and they're really run down. There's disgusting shit there—roaches on the floor and babies in diapers that haven't been changed in days. So I don't even hardly know what's fun to kids anymore. But I would have liked to have a mom, a dad, a dog, a white picket fence, and a family car.

I went from Florida to Ohio a lot. I would live with my mom for a while, and then she would move and I'd go to my aunt and uncle's and cousins. They're a real family. They act like a TV family. They eat dinner together at the same time every night and sit around and talk and share how their day was. They do things together on the weekends. They remind me of *The Waltons*—because my little cousins at night get out of their beds and go in everybody's room and say good night to them. Before I lived with them, I didn't have a family. I just had myself and my friends.

Last year I went back down to Florida to live with my mom. She thought she was ready to take care of me. She wasn't doing drugs anymore. She's been clean for over three years. But she still wasn't ever home. She did construction painting, and all she did was work and work and work. I wanted her to be eating dinner with me and taking on her responsibility as a parent. So I started hanging out with gangs because that was the first thing I was introduced to here. My aunt and uncle were two thousand miles away, in Ohio, so I didn't have their support.

I didn't join a gang in Florida, I just hung out with them. They were mostly Crips. But I also was with Folk Nation and knew Latin Queens. The gangs are all mixed down here. The kids are black, white, Puerto Rican. To be with them, I skipped school all the time. Sometimes I just didn't leave to go in the morning. My mom never knew 'cause she went to work early. She also didn't know that I got suspended because I would unplug the answering machine after she left. I was used to school being interesting in Ohio, and the teachers were better there. When I got down here, it was just, "Do this, do your work." So I would go to school tripping. It made everything so interesting.

The first time I smoked pot, I was nine. I thought it was a cigarette that my mom had left in the ashtray. But then when I got high with my baby-sitter when I was eleven, I said, "I know this feeling." I don't remember what I did, but it was fun. My friends and I used to drink Mad Dog and go to the park and get high. I tripped a bunch of times. I loved to get high. I lived for it. The one thing I can remember good about my mom was when she took me to the zoo. But that was when I was hallucinating. She's really never taken me there.

You know, there's no reason to get high. You can think of a million excuses as to why you think you want to or need to get high. Everybody knows there's other ways to deal with their problems. It didn't matter to me what drugs did to my family. All I could think about was getting high.

My mom sent me back up to Ohio because she couldn't cope with me and she wanted me out of trouble. My mom thinks that whoever she gives me to is responsible for me. I got over it a long time ago because I know how she thinks. I haven't accepted it, but I just don't let it get to me anymore.

When I was back up there this time, I was about twelve. I went and looked for the gang members and found 'em. They were Crips like in Florida. This time I joined the gang. It just felt normal to me because that's who I was used to hanging out with. I joined it for the family and because I fell into the wrong crowd.

You can choose to get beat in or sexed in. You only get blessed in if you've been in the gang before or something. If you get sexed in, they consider you a Crip ho [whore], and the gang will still give you love but no respect. I got beat in, which was the mistake of my life, but you know, it didn't matter to me at the time. I had to fight six guys and two girls at one time for three minutes. They were bigger than me, one guy was around sixteen, and I got the crap knocked out of me. I had a black eye and a busted lip. My nose was bleeding. So I told my aunt I got in a fight with one of my friends.

My nickname was Lil' Crazy, and I had a tattoo with it carved in my ankle. You get an OG when you're in the gang—mine was a guy who is an ex-boyfriend. There's things you learn from them by just being around and listening. Like I know how to sign, but now I don't like to. My boyfriend, who's in jail now, showed my little cousin how to do gang signs. That really pissed me off. He's only six years old, and he goes around wearing a blue bandana on his head and plays gangster. I hate it, and I used to yell at him for it. It may be OK for me, but I don't want him hanging out in a gang.

I knew a lot of Crips that told me to stay out of trouble and do well in school so I wouldn't end up like them. I had enough respect for the gang that I would do all that stuff they told me. But really the reason I did well was because I didn't want my aunt and uncle knowing I was in a gang. So I got straight A's, and I was on the honor roll and the drill team. Usually, I did listen to my aunt and uncle's advice because I respect them. I didn't have no respect for my

Signing a Crips star

mother, though, because of all the stuff that she had put me through. I wouldn't ever listen to her.

I really liked to destroy things. I've tried to figure out why, but I don't know. I tagged up anything I could find. We used to always tag the railroad trestle, writing Crip signs and stuff. I got in fights. Basically I stuck up for my gang.

That's the way you get respect. Like if somebody came up talking shit about my gang, I wasn't gonna ignore them. I was also in a couple gang fights, and all hell breaks loose. Sometimes, like two or three sets will come and fight a rival gang. After one I participated in, I will never do it again.

I am scared shitless of guns. Then, I would take a gun from one person to another. Now I won't touch them. That's because I went to seven friends' funerals in the nine months I was down in Florida. If I hadn't, I probably would have done a drive-by. My mom yells at me when I say this, but in my eyes, sometimes there's a purpose for drive-bys. That's the way some people handle their anger. People expect everybody to handle their anger in the same way, and what the hell, what would be the purpose of living if you do everything the same?

My aunt and uncle knew I had been getting in trouble, but they thought with all the funerals I had been to, I wouldn't want to be in a gang up there. Once they asked me, "Are you in a gang?" I said, "No—I already told you I wasn't going to do anything like that anymore." And they said OK. Then, one day my supposed best friend told my uncle. I came home, and he goes, "Pack your bags," and I was like, "What'd I do?" He said, "You're in a gang. You're not staying at my house." He and my aunt called my mom. At first she didn't want me to come back and live with her. She was doing her own thing. So they said, "If you don't take her, we are going to send her to Children's Services." She said no, don't do that. And the next week I found myself down here at my mom's house, and then two months after that, I was here at The Starting Place.

Coming here is the way for me to stay out of the gang. There's a couple other kids here who have been in gangs. But I'm the youngest. A lot of the kids here have drug problems and problems with their families. I didn't come here because of drugs. I told them in my interview I did them but if they told my mother, I wouldn't come to this program. Now I've been living here for four months. I really want to get out of here and go back up to Ohio. I miss my cousins and friends. When you've completed certain issues on your treatment plan, you go to the next phase and then you graduate. There are three parts, and I'm in Phase Two. I don't like it much, but it is teaching me how to check my feelings and stuff. I also go to school here and have individual and group therapy.

We have family sessions, too. I'll talk about when I was little nobody paid any attention when I was angry. My mom just thought I was cute and I was showing off. She never listened to me. I didn't know how to express my anger.

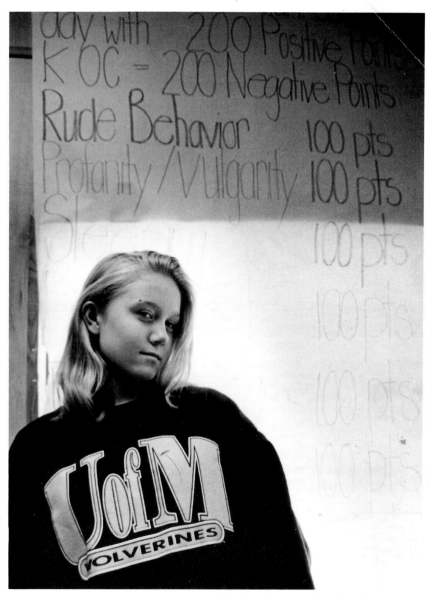

Brandy after getting "points" and put on status

That made me very angry 'cause I couldn't tell nobody I was angry. Once, I told my mom if she didn't stop pissing me off, I was gonna kill her. She thought I was being cute then, too.

Before I came in here, my mom thought I was still trying to show off. I thought if my mom found out about the gang, she would take me seriously. I looked at that reason for joining after I got in the gang. Every time I thought about it, it brought a smile to my face, like I can't wait till she finds out. I thought she might pay attention.

I still have a lot of anger from when I was a little kid. It's a combination of everything that happened when I was younger and stuff that still happens. In here, when you have rude behavior or do something wrong, you lose all privileges, like going to the movies or a football game. It's called status, and I've gotten put on it a lot. Like when I get really pissed off at someone and it just comes to me and I cuss them out. They teach you to do anger checks, so I'm starting to get along with people. Like when I first got here, I didn't like the big sibling they gave me. She was a Latin Queen—that's a rival gang. First we really hated each other, but now we get along fine.

All the therapists called me in one week and told me they were going to terminate me if I didn't do certain things. Can you imagine being in a room with four therapists? I guess they saw me slowing down, and they wanted to get me motivated. So I had to write a list of how my mother has hurt me and a list of how I've hurt other people. And I had to run a group session and talk about that stuff. In the group I did a psychodrama. You pick clients to play your family members, and you go into an isolated area while they work out how they're going to replay your past for you. Then you watch them play your past and you confront them as if they were your family members. They piss you off and you get to punch a bag. My mom was in the room the whole time. I was like, Oh shit, how am I going to do this? So I got to cuss my mother out in front of her and punch the bag. You know, I got a better rush when I started punching that bag than I did when I got high.

I also have to run a group with all the people here and explain my feelings about why I joined a gang. And I look at it now, and it was stupid and immature. There's a lot of things that I still like about the gangs, like they were there for me. But there's more that I don't like about them. Anybody that's involved with you is at risk. It may be a good decision at the time to join, but it ain't worth getting your ass beat and fucking up the rest of your life. It really affects you when you get older. It's like a tattoo—it's there for life.

So I am doing those things the therapists asked, but after I get out of this place, I never want to see another therapeutic assignment as long as I live. I guess it has taught me how to improve my relationships, like with my mom and her boyfriend, Tom. That's a good thing about this program. I'm getting along

Brandy and her mom having their photo taken together for the first time

more with her when I go on pass. Sometimes I go to help her and Tom at the Laundromat they run. She takes me to the mall like when we went to Glamour Shots. It was the first time we ever had our picture taken together.

I also like to go to church with my mom. Every morning when I wake up, I pray for my family and that I will keep myself together for the day. Then I pray at night, and I thank God for helping me keep myself together. Sometimes in

Brandy and her mother often go to church together now.

the middle of the day, I rehearse the serenity prayer in my head. I say, "God, grant me...," and I break it down to "Can I change the situation?" And if I can't, I accept it. You know, the only way I can change it is to have the courage to prevent it from happening in the future. Sometimes I reverse it: "God, grant me the serenity to accept the things *my mother* cannot change, for *her* to have the courage to change the things *she* can, and for *her* to have the wisdom to know the difference."

Now I have to figure out where to live when I leave here. I'll be able to say hello to my friends, but I can't hang out with them. And I'm scared to go back to Ohio. If you depart yourself from the gang, you can get violated. I have to decide whether I'm gonna live with my aunt and uncle and see my mom for the holidays or the other way around. I don't know what I'm going to do. I just got to figure that out. I would rather go to my school in Ohio. I wish I could put it on a trailer and move it here with all my friends. I want to be in two places, and I can't. But I think I want to live with my mom. I respect her now, and our trust and understanding is a lot better. Our ability to not scream at each other is better, too! I can say I love her, and I know she is trying harder.

You know, anybody would love to have someone to blame their problems on. I don't blame my mother. When she was around nine, she started drinking and skipping school. By about eleven, she started smoking weed. She told me she did it because she wanted to fit in. But my mom had a lot of responsibilities when she was a little kid. I mean, she was being a mother to her three younger sisters because my grandmother was an alcoholic. I know she was never really taught parenting skills when she was growing up. She was confused on that. She's not responsible for my actions; I am. I think I'm a strong person or, man, I would have killed myself by now from the stuff that I'm into. The more you live, the stronger you get. It's OK that I've had experiences that made me stronger. But I wish they would have been different ones.

Brandy has graduated from The Starting Place and is in outpatient therapy. She is living with her mother in Broward County, Florida.

Khmer Pride

My house was burned, people are dying
I struggled and crossed the many seas
Every step I took my stomach was emptied
My heart shattered unsatisfyingly

Why me, why us, why Cambodia
Why Khmer and Khmer fought each other
Why blood was shed, why skulls were scattered
Why me so far be not so near?

My fellow countrymen lend me your ears
Listen to those voices which scream in pain
Their lives may but not die in vain
Let us be awake to merge as one

Let us be Khmer JAYAVARMAN*
Behold of hope to free the Khmer soul
Be strong against wind like the bamboo tree untold
The reason it bends is to save its root

So now we are lost in the darkest storm
Alienated from home a million miles away
I hope to see that spring in May
When one day I will return to my homeland
For all my struggling ones, I will never hide
For I have in me the love of Khmer pride

—Saroeum Phoung

*Ancient Cambodian kings who were superior warriors and brought Buddhism, fairness, and hope to their people

ទឹកដីភ្នែកវាស្រុកខ្មែរ

សូរងង្រ្យម នាបទេះ
ព្យុះភ្លេងទុក្ខា
សរ្យងង្រ្យម ធ្លើ្យ
រងកម្ម សរ្យ្រនក
របេកផ្ទរុបថ្លឺ
ខ្លួនជំរ្កម្ល្ជ៉ារ
ព័ណមខ្មែរបាររបញ្ញរ
ទឹកដីភ្នែករវាញ្ញវ្យព
ឆ្យរុបរ្ចមគ្ន្រ
ចិត្ត្ក៊ម្យ ឃ្យ្រត
នោះ ណេវបីរ្បិម្រុយ
រ្យពឝ័ងជ្ជិរ្រប់យ៉ង
ខ្មែររេរ្យ្រខ្មែរ
អ្នក្ក្រុរ លើកការ៉ន
ន្ម្រភ្យពខ្ល្ង ខ្លស់
រ្យករ្យ ខ្ន ជ្ញ្រយ៉ង
ក្ក្ង្រពលគ់ខ្យ្រ
រ្រ្ញព្រ្ក្ស្មរ្យ្រង
សរ្ជ៉្យមរ្បរ្យ
រ្លវ្យ្រយ្រុយ៉ង់ ប៉ាន
ម៉នខ្ម្រ៉ រ្រុ្ខ
រ្យ្រន្ស្ក្ម្រ ្ត្រ
រ្ពតនោ ្ក៊្រ ចិ្ត្ត
រ្ម៉ន់ប៉ំ្រង ្ចរ្ក្រុ

ដ់្ក្រ្ម្ម្ង្ន្ន
ស្ម្យ្រ្រ្ម្ម្យ្រ្ន្រ្ន្ក
ខ្ញុ្រ្ក្ទឹកដីភ្នែក
ម្យ្រ្រ្សត្ន
ន៉ំ្រ្រ្រ្ក្រ្ប្គ្រ្ន
ច្ន្រ្ខ្ម្រ្រ្ធ្ម្ម
រ្រ្ន្ស្ន្រ្ម្រ្ក្ម្ម្ញ្រ
ចុ្ទ្រ្ជ្រ្ម្ត៉្រ
ខ្ម្រ្ម្ម្ម៉្រ្ម៉្រ្ន្ម្ម្រ
ព្ន្ម៉្ក្ម្រ្ម្រ
ច្រ្រ៉្រ្ម្ក្រ្ន្រ្យ្រ្ង
រ្រ្ស្ក្ម្ម្រ្ម្ម្ម្ក
ខ្ម្រ្ម្រ្ម្រ្ន្រ
ន្រ្ន្ម្ម្ន៉ខ្ម្រ
ក្រ្ត្ម្រ្ក្រ្ស្ន
ជ្រ្ត្ម្ម្រ្រ្ម៉្យ្រ្ចុ
ខ្ម្ម្ម្រ្រ្ម្ន្ង
ម្ម្ម្រ្ម៉្រ្ម្ម្ម្រ្ម្ម្ម
ច្រ្ម្ខ្ម្ន្ម្ន្ន្ម
ទ្ក្ម៉្ម្ស្ម្ន្ន្ម្ម្ម្រ
ម្រ្ម្រ្ត្ម្ន្ម្ត
ខ្ម្រ្ម្ន្ច្រ្រ្ន ស្ម្រ្ម
ខ្ម្រ្ម្រ្រ្ម្ម្ន
ម្រ្ក្ម្ម្រ្ក្ម្រ្ម្រ្ម្រ

ភ្ម្ម្ស្ម៉្រ្ម

Two

Surviving in Between

Ethnicity has been a motivation for membership, recruitment, and protection in gangs throughout the United States since the late 1700s, when Irish immigrants in Boston and New York banded together because they could not find work, due to discrimination. In the mid-1800s, numerous youth gangs were active in Philadelphia, and Chinese gangs emerged in California. By the 1920s, Mexican gangs were prolific in Los Angeles. And during the twenties in Chicago, where so many immigrants settled, Italian, Polish, African-American, Irish, Jewish, and Lithuanian gangs fought each other. Today, in cities throughout the country, there are Honduran, Nicaraguan, Cuban, Puerto Rican, Haitian, Jamaican, Cambodian, Vietnamese, and Samoan gangs, as well as rainbow gangs, which consist of several races and ethnicities.

When immigrant parents do not find a way to adapt to American society, their children are left to find their own solutions. About ten million immigrants entered the United States in the last decade, more than in any other ten-year period in American history. At least 31.8 million people in the United States speak a language other than English at home. And in urban public schools, one third of school-children speak a foreign language. Joining gangs is one way for immigrant kids to find a sense of their language, identity, and culture, which they may have left behind in their birth countries.

Saroeum Phoung (pronounced suh-ROME fong), twenty-two, left Cambodia when he was seven. After spending three years in Khmer Rouge war camps, his family then escaped to Thailand before coming to Boston. After getting out of the BRDs (Boston Red Dragons), he both participated in and was employed by ROCA, a multiracial intervention program for at-risk youth. During these interviews, Saroeum was under indictment for assault with a deadly weapon. Subsequently all charges have been dropped. He, his wife, Elizabeth, and their son, Sombatchey, live in Chelsea, Massachusetts.

Saroeum Phoung

We had a wonderful family when we first came to the U.S. We got here in August 1984—my four brothers, mother, father, and uncle. In November it started snowing. And my family had never seen snow. We went out and were throwing snowballs. The day my family arrived here was the day of my life.

We had no choice but to leave my country. There was war in Cambodia. There is a communist bullshit kind of thing. People were getting killed, and you didn't have food. It's like slavery. We had nothing over there. The Khmer Rouge thing, it was supposed to be a revolution to help the people. But instead it was to kill the people. People that have lighter skin get killed. My skin would be dead. And people who wear glasses, because that shows you are upper-class. And if you're in the Cambodian army, they kill your whole family.

My family was separated during the war. My brother Sarann, the oldest one, was forced to join the Khmer Rouge army to fight. I guess they killed a lot of people. That's what he told me. Like one day they had a festival, with good food and everything. The food was poisoned. He was able to escape. We lost him in 1975. Then in 1979 we found him. We were losing all our connections. My father didn't know where my mom was, and she was pregnant. He didn't trust anybody at that time. He loved me a lot because I was the youngest. So he took me to the front line when I was about three or four years old. The Khmer Rouge was shooting at the Cambodian army he was in. I watched my father get shot. He blanked out 'cause he lost a lot of blood. So all I was doing was crying out and calling him. And then he finally got back up. And he said, "I'm dizzy." Now when I talk to him about the war, he tells me why he brought me with him. He says, "If I took you with me and thought you would be killed, then I have anger to fight."

I also saw these brothers who tried to run away from the Khmer Rouge camp. They caught them—let them sleep nice and smoke and eat before they kill them. They tied them up, their feet and their hands together, and put a rope through a tall coconut tree and lifted them up. Then they would drop them. The whole town was invited to watch. And when you see that, you don't scream, you don't cry, you don't feel, you don't think. They want you to laugh about it. They say people that are against Angka, they deserve to be tortured. Angka is like a god and the government of Pol Pot. Pol Pot was the leader of Khmer Rouge.

I left my country in 1979. We didn't come from Cambodia right to here. We were in two Thai camps. People were just running all over the place. It's a lot of confusion—the war and everything, the hunger. First at the camps, it was people building your own house and you grow your own things. But then it's like prison. The Thai government built a fence around the camp and had soldiers. I was there for about five years. Then we went to the Philippines, and we got here.

My parents and some older folks would not talk about what happened in Cambodia. They just keep it to themselves. That's why they get crazy. Our family didn't talk about it. I don't talk to anybody. My father don't talk to anybody. Everybody just shut their mouth. Before, we stuck together as a family. And when we came to this country, like damn, we're in the land of making a dream come true. And then it was like we split. I didn't understand it. I was a kid.

My mother worked two jobs when we came here. She worked really hard to get her family in the right place, trying to save some money for us to go to school. All she wanted was my father to stay home, go to school, and learn some English. And he doesn't do that. He's an alcoholic. I can't say nothing but the truth. He drinks a lot, and he likes to gamble. And I have two brothers who do, too. My father went out to get drunk and gamble and took all the money that my mother was trying to save. It was about forty thousand dollars, and he just wasted it in six months. We were supposed to buy a house. That must have been hell. Every penny earned was through her energy and sweat.

Just comes a time when a lot of things hit me at once. I got problems at home. My mother had it with my father. My parents don't get along with each other and filed for divorce. I didn't talk to anybody about the problems at home. It was an Asian traditional kind of thing. I asked my mom, "Why is everything this way?" And I remember clearly my mother said, "When you get older, you'll understand."

A lot of things are different over here. In Cambodia, we respect older people more than in this country. When we walk past them, we put ourselves lower.

Saroeum with his mother, wife, and son

21

And in the Asian family, like I say, we don't communicate and you never attempt to show feelings. When you're parents, you don't say to your kid, "Son, I love you a lot. I hope you do good." I was waiting for my mom to say that for a long time. She tried, and I know deep inside of her she loves me and cares for me. But sometimes she doesn't show it. And Cambodian culture, it's not like the American family. I don't give my mom a kiss before I go to school or say, "How you doing, Mom?" We just go to school. The feeling never shows through to a son or daughter from their parents.

Also, nobody in my family really spoke English when we got here. So when I went to school, I didn't understand anything the teachers were telling me. I was dressed like a girl. But I didn't know it. I lived in East Boston, where the majority of people are Italian and white. And when I walked home, kids would swear at me, calling me names like "gook." Some of them were holding Christ in their lives and still called me gook. And they used to call me "you Chinese this and that." And I want to say to these people, "You're fucking stupid—I'm not even Chinese. So what does this have to do with me?"

Once these guys came up to me with hockey sticks. I was playing video games with the money I got for turning in cans. I was about fourteen, and they were about eighteen. They spit at me right in my face. I don't really say anything because I don't speak the language. So I keep playing and laughed with my friends, and this guy came over and smushed his cigarette in my favorite jacket and burned a hole, and I didn't have much clothes when I came here. The other guys smacked me in the head. So I tell my friend it's not worth it. And I walk home. I didn't tell my parents what was going on.

I couldn't explain it to my mom. If I told her they beat the shit out of me on the way home from school, she would tell me to shut up and I was a trouble-maker. And then you have the people that speak English who don't understand you at school. Like you say, "I came from Cambodia," and they would say, "Where?" You have to point to the map. So in school they don't understand where I'm from. At home my mother don't understand what kind of situation I'm facing. If she did, she wasn't ready to deal with it.

That's when I started to hang out with guys in my neighborhood. It started out as a racial thing. You come to this country, people look at you differently. Treat you like dirt. It makes you feel hopeless. So now where do people turn? Like me, I turned to a gang. These guys grew up in the same place and had the same experience. I'm sure that they got called gook. We're all in the same boat.

We weren't into alcohol; we didn't have guns. We were just kids hanging out. That's when I moved to Chelsea. I was about fourteen or fifteen.

I felt like I got lost between two identities when I got involved in the gang. Your family rejects you when you join a gang. And then you go out on the street and society reject you. You're living in American society, so you try to go with the flow. But in Cambodian culture, for example, you can't touch my head unless you're older than me. And if I go outside, people will say, "Hey, Saroeum," and tap my head. Sometimes it make you feel left out. You know, you say, Damn, they don't even respect my culture. And then when you go home, you bring the American society into the house, and then you get rejected there, too. When I came here, I didn't understand much about my culture or American culture. In a way, in the gang, we created our own culture.

It was totally different from gangs you've ever seen. I think the reason is, we weren't a gang because we wanted to be one—it just grew from a lot of love. It became a close family. Most of us have brothers in the gang. We would hardly take a beating from anybody. The reason is, if you were my brother, for example, and I see you get beat up, I'm not going to run. I'm going to go and help my brother.

And so the bond with the gang becomes stronger and, I guess, the identity with it. We were like ants. If something happens to one of us, we get in a group and try to find that person. And every time we walk on the street, people look at us weird. Basically, we grew up like one person. We were like a family, a government, a rule. Just a system for ourselves. We looked at the American people who were against our race. We have no clue what the hell they were doing to us. You don't play us out like that. We're going to tell you that we're here and we're staying. So we got to have some kind of a groundwork. I mean, I can't get a job. I can't do anything to get clean money. I can't sell drugs, because I'm not into drugs. So I have to do what we did. It's about, like, taking care of your family.

This time was difficult for my mother. She was there for me, but she was working hard and taking care of everyone. She's a good mother, but I think she was fed up with me. So she sent me down to live with my brother in Providence, Rhode Island. She didn't know he was into gangs. I went to school for one day down there and got kicked out. I lived in an apartment with fifteen other guys who all ended up in the gang. I was the youngest. There were three or four Asian gangs that came from California. We got in fights with them and with skinheads. It was for territory. We did different stuff, but we were not involved in drugs. Never. I think the reason is, for us, we used the gang as medicine. It's a positive energy in the bad. During those days we weren't breaking the law because that's how we took care of our friends.

Down there is when the whole activities changed and where we started the BRDs, Boston Red Dragons. Later, when we came back up to Boston, the police called us the Bloody Red Dragons. We would get together and talk about Cambodia on days when the sun would come out. We used Cambodian and American street language. Like someone in the gang, we call *poghma*, a close friend, or say, "What's up, homie?" Sometimes I feel, Damn, I never had a chance to meet those kind of people through a positive way. I wish I didn't have to go through the gang stuff in order to get to know them and find that love among ourselves. It's impossible to find that kind of love. We didn't mean to be negative, but sometimes society forced us to be.

It was because we had no money, no support, no nothing. These are kids who have no high school diploma and can't get a job. So we did a lot of house invasions for money and jewelry. The first one, I was at the front door by myself and four guys were at the back door. Two people had guns. I had a knife. I wasn't interested in a gun. I know it would help me at some point, but I know I have a really high temper. So I don't want to hold one. Nobody wanted to go to the front because they were scared. "OK," I say. "I'll go." I kicked the door and got hit with a baseball bat by the person inside. I was saying, Where are those motherfuckers? They finally break the back door and went in. We taped the people in the house, their mouths shut. We asked the guy who hit me, "Are you going to give us the money? Or we'll have to beat the shit out of you." And he said no. We pull his head up from the floor. One of my friends pulled out a gun and shot him through the earlobe. Then we got the money and got out of there. We would live on that money till there wasn't any, and then we would do it again. It freaked me out for a while. People think when you're in a gang, you can't feel anything, that you are just crazy young people running lost who are killing. Maniacs, like a cyclone. But there's a human young person. There's a human to me.

But during that time, there was no remorse. There was no time to say I'm sorry or to say forgive me. It was a time to survive. And that's when I was into the gang heavy. I was about seventeen. I came back to Boston. My street name was Tommy, for Tomahawk. I used to carry an ax with me. I didn't care if people knew I was in a gang. But if you messed with me, you knew. Around that time I could sometimes get work, like lifting trees. And I also started going back to school.

Molly offers Saroeum some advice.

My mother paid for a private school, Cathedral High. I went in and out of school. There I got a reputation as a gang member. I dress in street clothes, and most of the Asians wore normal stuff. I would have a red tag hanging from my pocket. I got respect after I brought a gun to school. It's a stupid way, but it also helped with a conflict I had with some kids. Some of my teachers tried to understand me and get me to laugh. Some of school I really liked. I had a good friend there, and she introduced me to Molly.

I was in a lot of trouble when I met Molly. Having a lot of fights. I remember having a shootout with some other gang. During that time it was just downhill. My friend was going to the program Molly ran called ROCA—it means "rock" in Spanish. It helps kids like me. She told Molly about me—that I painted and wrote poetry and that I was in a gang and in trouble. So Molly came to look for me. She just showed up on the basketball courts in Revere and introduced herself. She said, "Are you Saroeum Phoung? Do you have a street name you feel more comfortable to call you?" I told her she could call me Saroeum. So she tells me she did street outreach. During that time my ear is deaf. I was, like, I don't give a fuck about ROCA. And I don't give a shit about her. You know, She's a white lady, and she doesn't know shit about me.

I didn't put my trust in her right away because there were other people that had tried to help me from other programs. But then she kept showing up while I'm on the street, drinking a forty. She would show up in the middle of the night. I mean, this lady used to call me at school to see if I was there. I had a beeper then, so she used to beep me, and she gave me all her numbers to call. I really hated her at this time. I felt like taking a gun and blowing her head off. I didn't see that she was helping me. One of the things that did help is that she persevered.

She didn't see me as a parent would, their kid drinking on the street. She was looking at my brain. I wasn't just a figure of me being on the street. I was a figure of a young person who has a lot of talent. So she kept open to me and was pretty good at handling stuff, like when I would shut down or attack her. I told her I was in a gang and that my life was pretty boring and I wanted to belong to it less. And suddenly she asked, "Are you able to talk to your family about this?" I told her that my family is not really organized and they're all screwed up. Except my mom. And she can't take care of everybody.

She gave me a ride and said, "You are talking about a lot of stuff which is good, and now I understand some of it." Then she asked me, "Saroeum, do you want to live or do you want to die?" And nobody had ever asked me that, and it's tricky and weird. I say everybody's born and they want to live. I don't want to die. If I wanted to die, I would have killed myself a long time ago. And after a while she said, "You're not about living, because you're about dying." She said, "You have the decision and the answers inside of you. But you're afraid to put it out on the table and say that you're a man that can take care of yourself and that it's about a positive thing." And during that night, I was crying. It was so personal and touched me. I never had somebody to really listen to me. She said it's OK to cry. As a gang member I hardly see anybody cry. I told her, "Damn, I can't believe I'm crying in front of a white lady."

The next day I could see myself start to think about making a change. Yeah, in just one day. The whole day passed, and I figure we both don't remember anything about it. I went over to a friend's house for a party, and we were drinking and there were guns on the wall. Molly showed up again. She asked to be invited in to talk to me. She took me outside and asked if I thought about what we were saying last night. And I was like, yeah. And at those times I began to put trust on her. It was like being in my gang. If I have to rob a bank or do a home invasion for my gang, I would do that. And for Molly it's the same thing. She believes in young people making a change. She did this on her own time, on her own will.

She reminded me to call her anytime, and she tried to put me back in school. My mom paid for me to go to school, but they were ready to kick me out. Molly talked to them and helped me get back in. She kept telling me that she wasn't there to put pressure on me. She was there to help me make a decision. She brought me a choice.

Between my junior and senior year, I was arrested twice. One was for a racial fight. It was between an American and Asian kid. Between gook and gringo. They press charges on me, saying I cut somebody with a knife on the street. Molly came and helped to get the whole thing mediated. The charges were dropped both times. But I stayed in jail the second time for a week, and if you're absent from school that long, you flunk the whole quarter.

So in my senior year I flunked two classes. The principal of my school said I couldn't graduate unless I made up the work and got a B and an A average. I had to study using a Kmai dictionary. I could learn to speak English on the street, but I would flunk if I had to write a test. Then I also read a lot of books about the Khmer Rouge. I ask a lot of people who were in and out of Cambodia. Because there is nothing in school about our culture. I talked to my history teacher and said every year there's a black history month and so I figure they should have a Cambodian month. Then she let me talk to my whole class. I told them where I lived and how we came here because of the war. I showed the video *The Killing Fields*. And now they know on the map where my country is and could understand where I came from. They don't look at me that I'm just another Asian guy. We're Asian but, you know, Chinese, Vietnamese, we all have different experiences.

So instead of hanging out, I would read a lot. I wrote a lot of poetry, too. And I would do painting, mostly landscapes and sunsets of my country. It was peaceful, like meditation, and put me in a good mood. So when I came home, I had a lot of energy to do work. I did a big painting and I was surprised how good I was. I felt good about it. The teacher thought I could go to art school someday. I worked really hard during that time. It was a tough year to finish school, but I showed I could make it.

When I graduated, Molly was there. My parents didn't come. I guess at that time they didn't care. If it had been my son, I would be damn sure to be there unless I was in prison. I was pretty mad, and I wasn't going to go. But Molly said they must have had something to do. And when I got up to get my diploma, everybody got up and said, "Gang member." It was a positive kind of thing. I guess they were proud of me somehow. I was all ready to cry. I said to my professor, I have it, I have it! I was like, damn, I accomplished something.

I was going to ROCA while I was finishing school, and after school I started to work there. It's a multiracial kind of place. The kids are involved running it, not just adults. I do street outreach near schools and talk to kids and see what's up. I also teach volleyball and kick boxing. My father taught me Cambodian kick boxing. I teach a more American kind of kick boxing, not as dangerous. It's good to teach kids self-defense. When I teach, I also talk to the kids. I find out if they show up at school. I tell them don't drink, don't smoke, and if they have family problems and can't talk to anybody, to come and talk to me. And we do.

I was a junior when I met Elizabeth, my wife, at school. She also worked at ROCA. She had problems, too, but she still was with me. She's Cambodian but

Saroeum teaching kick boxing at ROCA

Holding his son, Sombatchey

was never in a gang or anything. She's a tough lady even though she's quiet most of the time. And you know, she would buy me books, pencil, pens for my study. Elizabeth and I, we went through everything together. Now we have a son.

His name is Sombatchey, and he is almost two. When Elizabeth was pregnant, my friends told me to go to a good American doctor for an abortion because I couldn't take care of him. I proved them wrong. And I guess the kid really pulled me out from the street. I was feeling like any fool can make a baby, but it takes a real man to raise a child. I'm lucky to be his dad, and I'm sure his mom feels the same way. I tell my wife it's up to him to make his own choices. I could tell my kid the street is bad, but I have to give him the definition of it. If I don't tell him, he's going to want to try to see how bad it is.

Being a father myself, sometimes I can now relate to my father. I know he loves all of us, but because of the war, he's done a lot of bad things to my mom.

But my parents both have a place for me. So I try to help my family now. I talk to my younger brother Vichet. He's fifteen and at the age of going crazy, being in gangs. He didn't have any older brothers looking after him, because we all had our own families. So I try to tell him, like about AIDS when he goes to get a tattoo. My whole family relies heavy on me. My mother trusts me the most. I guess because I got out of the gang and finished school.

It's a lot of responsibility to help them, and now I have to think of my own family. I don't want my son to be too Americanized. You know, I think when you are, you're lost. And you're never going to look back and say I'm Asian. I think that education can help. It is definitely the answer to all kinds of problems.

That's why I tell Elizabeth go to school. Cambodian women are supposed to stay home, and it's sad we're not educating our women. She's almost graduating from college, and I'm not even in college yet. I'm looking forward to going, but I feel like I have a degree. It's being an ex–gang member. It's different from Harvard, but not many people have the degree that I have. Because some people get into the gang and never get out.

I want a strong future, but sometimes I have that feeling of going back to the street. I almost slipped through the edge and said, "Damn, let's go back to the gang." Because it made me feel warm. People don't reject you; they want you. But it's a different feeling now. Like using a gun, then you don't even think twice. Now you step back, and that's the difficult part—you can't do it. Now I think about it and there's a lot of fear.

There are people that still look at me like a gang member. And some people tell me, "Saroeum, you'll never make it." Those are the people that make a challenge for me to go on. And it's an irony. Because see, if I give up now, it tells all those kids who I've worked with that there's no way out.

I feel really fortunate to be here, just to live, to breathe the air every day. To see my family and my kid. I appreciate some part of my life. When I was in the gang, I was in what you call the fast lane. And I like quiet places, not so much city life. I want to see a sunset in Cambodia again and take my family back there. I want my son to see what I don't see. Because my country used to be peaceful, before the war. But I was a kid when the war happened, and what I see is the bombing, shooting, the killing. Sometimes I think probably it's like a dream. I wake up and suddenly it's all gone. But I think if I go to Cambodia right now, I'd be happy and feel more strong. I think I missed part of my life and a piece of me somewhere. And I want to get that piece.

Saroeum holding a painting he did of a Cambodian sunset

I tell Molly a lot and Elizabeth, too, I want to go to college and start writing. And the message, if I was going to write my own book, is that you don't have to be Asian to face this kind of problem with gangs. You don't have to be black, or white, or Latino. It could be anybody who can relate to the story I'm telling. I would want to get across there is always a choice for people who are involved in a gang. Don't wait until it's too, too deep. Like kill twenty people and go to jail and never get out. Wake up and think about yourself and where the hell you are at right now. See people like Molly inspire people like me. And it takes—what is the word? It takes a whole village to raise one child. It's true. I'm that one kid.

Saroeum has a new son and is employed by Streetworkers (see chapter 9), an outreach and intervention program for gang youths. He is also taking courses through the College of Public Community Service at the University of Massachusetts.

I don't know how to start. I'm a TNS baby, Noone knows ecxept Meli. She told me not to join but, I had to look tuff. Any way everyone is awayz picking on me!! So for sure I had to find a way to as I said before act tuff. Now I'm in it I don't have to be tuff my new friends do that for me

Gotta go peace out,

T.N.S.   OBG

ELENA

---

this is the end of OBG's (My) first week in T.N.S. didn't have to do any-thing wrong. I'm starting a new way of life or so I did last week. I feel very deprest. part of my depresion is cause I can't tell my mom I'm in a gang cause she'll split me. It's been alright I orcourse have had to fight, but only 4rhonor. My other part of my depresion is my boyfriend I'm having lots of problems with him.

tell you more later, Peace out,

ELENA

...time goes on I write less in my note-book. I'm wishing I had never got into this gang. Now I think twice ~~after~~ before stepping a foot out my front door cause alot of people got beef for me. My friend Maria is trying to talk plucky into letting me go but she has to be slow about it cause they'll split her back!!! I talked to gorge he said that a I.M.P.G. (I.M.P. Girl) was looking for me to cap me. So I met her behind the mall and we faught it out. I had to show my colors today!!! It truly is hard

Peace out,

ELENA

TNS is full of crap

They are letting me go slowly by burly. I hope. cause I been getting tricked lately. they say if I want to be let go I got to be walked-out it takes twice as much time than to be walkedin. and that takes 4 min.

Peace out,

ELENA

TNS going out the "94"!!!

Well now I go to L.H.I. and the first 3 weeks I inprooved my grades 45% thank GOD!!! Maria comes to this school to and I have her in most classes.

With so much
LOVE,

ELENA

P.S. New life for the new year

THREE

Really Protected

Teenagers and children often join gangs for protection. They want to be able to walk down their street or go to school without being afraid or harassed. With fifteen American children killed by handguns each day, kids' lives are exposed to more violence than ever before. Today, many children see their friends, their family members, or strangers abused, shot, stabbed, or arrested, often from gang violence. In urban neighborhoods, over 80 percent of childhood deaths are from shootings. But murders of and by juveniles have also spread to smaller cities and towns such as Duluth, Fresno, Wichita, and Davenport. While some sources suggest that homicide rates for adults in the United States are dropping, murder rates for youths ages fourteen through seventeen have tripled in the last ten years. It is a common belief among adolescents that they are in more danger from other teens than they are from adults.

Thirteen-year-old Elena Rojas (the name is a pseudonym) belonged to the gang TNS, Take No Shit, which she joined for protection. She lives in Miami, Florida, with her Cuban-born mother, stepfather, and baby sister. She attends Little Havana Institute, an alternative school for at-risk youths. Her mother did not know she had been in a gang until she requested permission to be interviewed for this book.

Elena Rojas

I've known about gangs since I was little because I never lived in a good neighborhood. Yeah, like you would go out, and all the gangs would rub your head and go like, "What's up, honey?" Then it wasn't as bad, you know. Gang members would stick to their own neighborhood and not go over and look for a fight. It was like everybody from that neighborhood got along with them. They didn't have any problems. So I learned a lot about the street on my own, and then my mom, you know, she was raised in a tough neighborhood, so she told me a lot.

My mom came to Miami from Cuba when she was thirteen. She hung out on the streets, but she was raised in a good home. My grandmother used to take care of her. She wasn't a problem child or a troublemaker. But she left home by the time she was seventeen because she couldn't stand my grandfather anymore. He was a drunk and abused her. My grandma and my mom told me about it, and I didn't want to believe them because I was like the eyes of my grandfather. He really loved me. After I saw him drunk, though, I understood why they told me.

My mom is very open with me, as I am usually with her. When she was young, she did a lot of drugs. She told me about it since I was eight. She said, "In case anybody comes up to you and tells you this about your mother, you

Elena with her family in their backyard

already know." When she tells me, like when she was in jail for seven months because of the drugs, it helps me understand more the way I should be. My aunt and grandmother helped her get out of doing drugs. By the time I was born, she had been clean for a couple of years.

My dad left right after I was born, so I didn't know him. My mother and me, we have our differences, but we always come out understanding each other. She's a good mother, and now she's married to my stepdad. I'm lucky because most kids don't get along with their stepparents. I have a great relationship with him because he takes care of me like the father I never had. That really helps in giving me like a push, to try my best.

I knew I had everything I needed to survive. But there's many reasons why people join gangs, like they're getting picked on. I have an acquaintance who was getting picked on by a gang that kept saying, "You're going to get your ass beat," so he joined the rival gang. In the gang I was in, the youngest girl was eight. She joined because her mother used to beat on her and she was suffering a lot. It's not that the gang members will protect them from their parents, but they think getting in a gang is going to make them stronger and their parents weaker, in a way. You have the strength 'cause you know how to use a gun and you have delinquent buddies in the street. Sometimes you're just having problems with somebody. I'm a good example that you don't always join 'cause of your family.

It was just 'cause of this one guy, my boyfriend Caesar, I joined TNS. He was a sweet talker, and that works with me. He was sixteen when we were going out and I was twelve. He started talking to me—"Oh, can I have your phone number?"—the whole routine as usual. He's about five-nine, and he used to do weights. He wasn't in a gang, but he hung out on the street and stuff. I cared a lot about him. But whenever he would get mad, he'd take it out on me. Not just beating me up but screaming at me—hurting my feelings and calling me names. He would hit me in front of his friends sometimes by mistake. They would tell him to back off and say, "That's not right." Then he'd leave me alone. I can't believe I fell for all his stuff, about that he loved me. I have one letter from when he punched me and he's saying how sorry he was. He said, "Oh, just forget about it—I didn't mean to do it."

I knew when it was coming because his face would be stressed and look like nothing you had ever seen. One time he hit me on the face with his ring. I have a scar on my nose from it. I didn't cry 'cause that would sort of make it worse 'cause he would say, "If anybody knows . . ." and this and that. I also saw his dad beat on his stepmother. It was as if I was looking at Caesar in a mirror. Then when he hit me, I remembered back to his father. I tried to help him a lot. I would tell him let's go to a counselor or whatever, but he wouldn't budge. I stayed with him because I loved him.

I didn't want to tell my mom about Caesar, because I knew she would tell me to break up with him. She didn't suspect anything, because she knew I got in fights if someone pushed me and got on my nerves. Finally I told her, and she said it's better you're not with him. She'd always turn things around and make them look good. After I got really tired of the stuff he did, I broke up with him. And he said, "If you don't go back with me, I'm gonna go after you."

I was tired of being picked on. When I hung out with the people in the gang before I was in it, I felt safe. We were in all our classes together. I thought the girls from the gang could give me good advice because they know more about, like, trouble. I could have just had the gang protect me, 'cause they knew me. But I wanted them to really, really protect me, and I wanted to be feared.

Caesar was the main problem. But I also joined the gang because I wanted to have something that encouraged me to do anything, 'cause I really didn't feel like doing anything. I was depressed because of my boyfriend. So I thought, The hell with it—it will keep him away from me. He'll know who not to mess with. And I mean, in a way, it worked. It kept him away, and it gave me that feeling back of my wanting to do something.

I got walked in to TNS. You can slide in if you have a big brother or sister that's in the gang. I got walked in by a line of girls. You walk down the line from one to the other one, and they stand five feet away from each other. When you get to the next person, they beat you up. They beat me up for four minutes. It went fine. Just my back was bruised and three ribs. They don't do anything to your face so your parents don't know. I guess it wasn't as scary for me as for most people because I was used to it from my boyfriend.

TNS is black and Latins, you know, mostly Hispanic—like Colombian, Puerto Rican, Cuban, Dominican, and Nica [Nicaraguan]. There were little branches, about sixteen, hooked up to one big gang. In ours there were about thirty-five people. The oldest was turning twenty-two. We spoke mostly Spanish but English, too. Like we say, "What's up?" or "¿Hoy, que vola?" And there are good things about gangs. You're protected. You have friends. They always watch your back. Well, the gang I was in, they were faithful. Some of the things are like what your family teaches you. To be honest. We had fun together and would go to Bayside. It's a nice place here in Miami. We would wear red and white bandanas in our hair. And the guys had red and white boxers. Mostly we were known as fighters and had a lot of territory. The gang we fought with the most also had some American kids—white kids. They're called INP [International Posse].

I have a friend that joined INP because of the drugs and guns. You get things so much cheaper. In TNS we didn't really do drugs. I didn't 'cause I know they mess up your life. I mean in a way I was already messed up, but I didn't wanna go crazy. And my mom was a recovering addict, so I really listened when she told me don't do that. There's some things like that I will never do 'cause my mom tells me not to. There's some things that later on in life I will do, and then there's some that I do whenever I want—like holding a gun.

You can get guns given to you for free. They're stolen—they'll just give them to you. About 50 percent of us had guns. I held a gun plenty of times, but I never had to use it. We used to put it inside the back of our pants. We would keep one bullet in the gun and keep it two shots away from where the bullet was. We would have the safety on, so I felt fine. It didn't bother me, because you get used to it after a while. But it's nothing I want to do again.

I was in three drive-bys. You get scared the first time 'cause it happens fast. It's not like they stop, get their guns ready, and start shooting at you. You don't have time to do what you want. They're passing by fast. Once my friend Sarai brought a gun to school. They only have a metal detector once a year when you least expect it. They think that's gonna help. That day there was a drive-by right outside of school. Another one of our friends got shot and died on the scene in front of me. She was twelve. The whole gang was at the funeral. Her mom wasn't the strong type. She didn't say anything to her daughter about being in a gang. If my mom knew, she would have told me, "No, you can't be in that."

Hugging her mother

When I was in TNS, Caesar stopped bothering me. But I couldn't stand people getting shot and hurt on account of protecting me and other gang members. I had problems with one of the INP members who was really dangerous. She had been convicted of first-degree murder and got out. She'd call me up and say she was TNSK, which means TNS killer. I didn't want anyone coming to my house to fight because my little sister might get hurt. So I asked the leader to get out. My friend's cousin was his best friend, so he asked for me first. He said, "I'll think about it." Then he talked to me. "Is it true—do you want to get out?" I was in TNS for only three months, but I told him yes. He asked me a lot of questions, and when I told him I don't want to do this, he said he wouldn't question me—it was fine. I think he was nice—because I could have gotten shot or hurt when I left. And he told me, "Look, if you have any problems with Caesar, if you need anything, call me." Caesar knew and never bothered me.

When I was still in TNS, it hurt me that I couldn't tell anybody from my family about being in the gang. I couldn't stand keeping it away from my mother, and I always had to invent something. Like when I got a black eye

Elena and her friend Maria

once. She would ask me, "Why aren't you the same person you were before?" She would start crying and say, "I know you're hiding something from me and you don't want to tell me." It was like a skeleton in my closet. I didn't tell her about TNS because I didn't want to hurt her.

I got out also because I didn't want to get caught. Before, I thought, Well, a lot of my friends have been to juvenile hall, so if they catch me, they catch me. But I didn't want a criminal record. It affects you when you grow up. If you go and ask all of the people I know in a gang, "Do you really like to be known as a criminal?" they'll tell you no. It's just that they're being picked on or their parents are always fighting.

My mother knew I was having problems, but she still didn't know about TNS. She told me that if I got in more fights, she'd take me out of school and put me in another one. And she wanted me to go to a better school. So she got me into the Little Havana Institute. It's a small school, and I like my friends there, like Maria, who helped me out of the gang. And Caesar doesn't know what school I'm at.

I probably wouldn't have gone back to the gang, but this school helped me make up my mind to not go back. My Spanish teacher there is the first one who knew I was in a gang. One day he asked me why I was wearing TNS colors. I said, "You know TNS?" And he said, "Yeah, are you a TNS?" I said, "No, I used to be." He said, "You know there's a TNS who got killed and died?" I said, "Yeah, I know." So we started talking a lot. And he was the only one who knew about me being in a gang except for Martha Young. She's my principal.

I can talk to Martha about my problems. I told her about my boyfriend and TNS. I also have a counselor I talk to who's really sweet and helps me a lot. The school gives me a motive to work 'cause in most schools they say, "Here's the

Little Havana Institute principal Martha Young takes Elena's Valentine's Day photo.

work" and you do whatever you want with it. You throw it away; you get an F. Too bad, you know? And here they tell you, "Look—if you get good grades, you could go places, to college," and they have special classes to help you. Now I want to get my diploma and go to college. I like animals and medicine, and I want to be a veterinarian. And now when I go home, I do my homework and take care of my little sister, Rebecca, because my mom and dad are at work. I play with her, and my grandmother comes over to visit us. Sometimes I write in my journal, like when I don't have anything else to do.

If Rebecca ever tried to get into a gang, I would stop her and show her my journal. I'd tell her what it's about and let her see the scars. For little kids like her, I would like to clean up my neighborhood. Kids could play on the street, and there'd be no gangs around. It would make it a lot easier for everybody.

If I could, I would tell someone, "If you get a chance to be in a gang, don't do it." First of all it will ruin your life. You never know if you are gonna get shot or stabbed, if you're gonna die or get put in jail. You have to be very strong to go through what people go through in a gang. Just stay in school; just study a lot. Get called a nerd as many times as you have to, but stay out of the gang. I wish they could get the gangs all over the United States and put them in a camp together—'cause most of the time when people get killed, it's one gang

Taking care of her little sister, Rebecca

Elena is glad to be out of her gang.

against the other. So they would have to live together for at least a couple of years and learn how to get along.

You know, most adults know more about life than they give. But my mom gives me the idea that I can trust her. She needs me to be the person I am inside, who loves children and helping people. When she gives me straight advice and I use it, everything goes well. But like with joining the gang, I did what I wanted for myself. If I didn't have her, I'd still probably be in juvenile hall and in that gang.

So I would like to tell all the parents, first look at the mistakes that they've made in their lives and give their kids as much understanding as they can. Listen to them, 'cause kids like to be listened to. See if they pay enough attention to their kids and spend as much time with them as they can. What most kids need is love and attention and someone to care for them. I have that.

Elena is in eighth grade and still at the Little Havana Institute. She is now getting all A's.

fear hate anger intolerance injustice inequality poverty illiteracy anxiety loss death murder illness guns war destruction suicide alcoholism addiction drugs POLICE politics bureaucracy red tape debt solitude loneliness gangs violence ashamed shame frightened upset tears worried scared unhappy depression terrified horrified ruthless dreading uneager guilty panic beaten outcast downcast cracked crackhead danger mad sorrow grief confused driven to the brink......   i'm not going to give up, are you?

—*Anonymous Boston City Year member*
First published in Moccasins 1994, *a collection of writing from City Year members*

City Year was created as a model national service program. In cities such as Boston, where the program started, young adults from diverse backgrounds spend a year doing full-time community service, helping to prepare themselves for their future and allowing them to begin contributing to their communities.

FOUR

Who You Fall in With

The need to belong to a group, to conform to a neighborhood, has always been a strong reason to join a gang. Simply living in certain neighborhoods places kids at risk of gang involvement. Many urban communities come with their own set of rules, a strict code of the streets, provoked and perpetuated by violence. At an early age, youths are conditioned to resolve disputes by fighting. If they don't, they risk losing respect, an essential commodity on the streets and in gangs.

Sixteen-year-old Patrick (the name is a pseudonym) lives with his mother and younger sister in a predominantly Irish urban neighborhood. Irish youth gangs are often fiercely loyal and cautious about their turf, and by request, this chapter omits Patrick's real name, his face, and specifically where he lives. Patrick's world is clearly a violent one, and like many of the kids in it, he is inclined to fight often. While he is protective about his neighborhood, he wants to leave—to escape the drugs, crime, and poverty. With the help of Hewitt Joyner III from Streetworkers (interviewed chapter 9) he began to improve his life, including enrolling in a GED program at an alternative school for at-risk kids.

Patrick

Where I live, everybody knows each other. It's pretty small. My mother grew up here, and I think her parents did, too. She's on SSI [Supplementary Security Income]. She can't work from health problems. My father doesn't live with us. Things just didn't work out for my parents. He gave me money once in a while, but that's about it. He wasn't a father. If he had been around more, I would have been out of the projects, living in a nice house right now. I wouldn't have been hanging out with the same guys. I guess if you are around good people, you're more than likely gonna be a good person. If you're around bad people, you're more than likely gonna be a bad person. It depends on who you fall in with.

I hang out with the guys in town because it's where we live. All of them aren't 100 percent Irish, but they mostly are. But I got no clue what a gang is. It could be anything. Look it up in the dictionary. There could be good gangs like the groups that are against drugs. Or I guess you could say, like, them angel guys, Guardian Angels. If you go up to the main street at night, you see all kind of kids hanging out there. I can walk there by myself and say, "What's up?" and no one would fuck with me. When I go somewhere with my friends and they have a problem with other guys, we fight them.

I should have been with kids more my own age—like playing baseball or whatever. But when I was nine or so, the guys I was with were twelve, thirteen, fourteen. That was through Mark, actually. He was like my big brother. When I was little, he sort of protected me. He's Irish–Puerto Rican. But we looked at it that he didn't live with his father, who's Puerto Rican. He lived with his mother, who's Irish. Everyone in town knew him because he grew up with us. He'd be about twenty now. But he's dead. He shot himself in the head last year in my building.

I guess I grew up a little too fast. Since I was the youngest, my friends tried to toughen me up, bustin' my balls. They never went to school, they're fuck-ups. By the time I was thirteen, I used to do all kinds of shit with them. I used to break into cars like crazy. That was my big thing when I was a little kid. The guys I was with when I was little are the ones I see now. But, after I was around twelve or thirteen, I hung out with another crew. Then those guys fucked me up.

Someone had robbed my house, and my mother start blaming people. So they made me fight this kid, one on one. I kicked his ass, so they all jumped me, dragged me on the cement, and stomped on my skull for about fifteen minutes. They gave me three skull fractures, a broken arm, and I almost lost my eyesight in one eye. I guess then I learned the hard way not to trust anybody. You don't rely on anyone but yourself. Most of that crew broke up. But when I see them, I still say, "Hey what's up? How you doing?" It's better to pretend someone's your friend than show them you're their enemy.

I don't think I've ever walked away from a fight. If someone's being a punk and he wants to fight me, I'll fight. I'm not going to stand there and let them bitch me around. We usually don't fight with weapons, but we all have them. It's better to keep them in your house. You don't want to bring heat to the street. You don't want to get beat with a gun charge and have all kinds of shit going through your whole town. It's usually head smart here. Most of the crimes are organized. People know stuff, but they tend to keep their mouths shut. See no evil, hear no evil, speak no evil. If you say anything, you're considered a snitch, and then watch your back.

The guys I hung out with, we used to make money by all different types of scams. And I guess you could say robberies. Here, they just rob the upper class. I don't have anything against the upper class, but they have big cabbage [money]. I've only robbed one house. We'd usually rob some dude walking down the street with a camcorder in his hand. You go over and punch his teeth

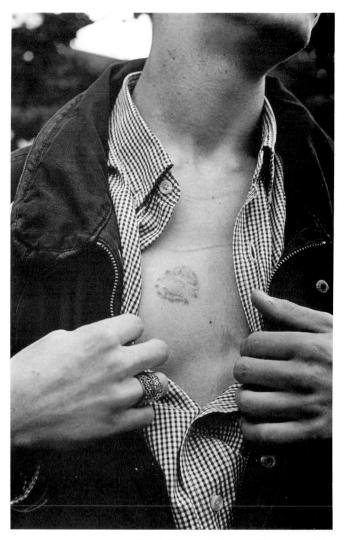

Patrick showing the bite mark he got in a fight

in, take it, and you sell it for like six bills. I'd like to forget about that stuff I did. But I actually enjoy hustling people, doing scams. Mostly my friends now aren't into stealing—they're into selling drugs. It's where the money is. That's what broke the trust with my friends. Drugs changed them, and drugs changed me, too.

I started experimenting with this and that, like angel dust and acid. It was easy to get. At first I actually used to do better in school when I was stoned. But after I got into acid, it took a couple of scruples away from me. I fell down the stairs once when I was high and got a compressed fracture in my back. Then I started taking painkillers. I don't know what they were, but they fucked me up.

Patrick in a neighborhood park

They were strong. They only gave me ten of them, but I ended up eating all of them. I just snapped. I was going crazy. My mother found me and took me to the hospital. I don't remember what happened.

When I came to, I was like, Whoa, whoa. I was put on machines. I looked around, and my mother wasn't there. So I ripped them off of me and left the hospital. The second time I OD'd, I had just broken up with this girl. So I thought I'd OD again. I started with about two, then four pills, painkillers. Then before I knew it, I ended up eating like thirty pills. They said I tried to commit suicide. I ended up in the hospital again with a tube up my nose and going down my throat. I think if I hadn't been fucked up, I wouldn't have eaten all those pills. I just wanted to get high. But I ended up in the cuckoo house, and after that they finally realized I needed rehab.

I went to a lot of rehabs, but I kept leaving and getting into fights. I didn't go to school the whole year, 'cause I had so many other things to worry about. When I stopped doing drugs is when I went to AA [Alcoholics Anonymous]. I got a sponsor and started going to meetings every day. I came to a point where

I said, "My name's Patrick, and I'm an addict." Then I knew what was up.

My mother told me when we got in a fight, "I can't deal with you anymore." We were always fighting. I love her, because she's my mother, but I don't like her. And my teachers didn't know what to do with me when I was high. I was going to an alternative school then. Finally they called in Hewitt. I used to get kicked out of school, and he used to come and take me out of class and say, "What's up?" The guy opened up to me a lot. He told me a lot of shit about himself, and usually they ask you but you can't know about them. He's a good guy. He's helped me a lot. I respect his advice. But I do my own thing if I want to.

Even though I wasn't doing as many drugs, I still got into fights, and Hewitt had to help me out. Because when I was in my other school, there was this fight. It wasn't racial, but they said it was. Everyone around here is pretty racist. They get it just from the town. Five years ago there was only one black guy living here. Now it's all Chinese, Puerto Ricans, and Haitians. They're moving in like crazy, and the town's disgusted. I don't think I'm racist. I have a couple of black friends. But you just hear it so much that if I was in a fight with a black kid, just from anger, I'd probably say nigger. I believe everyone has racist tendencies, everybody.

After school four black kids, two I knew, were playing basketball against four white kids, friends from the projects. The whole game, they were like, "White men can't jump." This little kid started playing rough with me. It happened a couple times, and three strikes, you're out. So I got in a fight with him. I grabbed him by his throat and then let him go. Some Puerto Rican kid came and smacked me. My friends were tripping at the time, and one says, "Oh, that's how it's going to be?" And he knocked down the kid I had choked. Then it happened so fast—everybody was fighting. I turned around, and all these kids were lying on the ground. They had to call an ambulance for two of the kids. The police came, and then I heard all this racial shit. "You cannot fight an immigrant or something different besides a white guy, or you get slapped with a racial charge." So I got thrown out of school, and they pressed charges against me.

I found out my teachers weren't behind me, only Hewitt and my mom. You know, my friends, they might have my back, but they're not going to take care of me. I didn't snitch on them because I didn't want to see them get screwed. They already have civil rights shit on them and long records. I thought the court was just going to slap me on the wrist. Then they hit me with assault with a dangerous weapon and civil rights charges. Hewitt came to court and got the charges dropped. I didn't have a weapon, and I don't think it was a racial thing. But I'm on probation. I have to go to a psychiatrist every week. I'd rather not, but I'm court-ordered. I have to be in school every day and work in the afternoons. I just have a year and a half to go—as long as I don't crack up! Now I really don't trust anyone but myself. But I guess I trust Hewitt. I'd pay him back if I could, but how could I? He gave me my freedom.

I stopped hanging out with my friends as much. It's not hard to not be with them. I see them bustin' out with H, and that's nasty. I still go with my friends. Don't think I shut them off. I'm just not really with them. They're losers. That's why I try to have girlfriends, so I don't have to go with them. Girls are fun, and I want to be with new people, somebody I can build a life with. But I don't like the girls from here. They're already starting to be junkies. See, at fifteen you smoke weed, sixteen you drink, at eighteen they're popping pills, nineteen they're doing coke, twenty they're coke whores, and by twenty-one they got the virus. I don't like girls that fight or don't want to go to school or do anything with themselves. I like my girls sweet and smart. Like one of my girlfriends, she could be anything, and she's in college.

Now I'm at a school working on my GED. I graduate in May. I want to work in computers or go to trade school for refrigeration, like my father. I want to get a good job, good pay, kick back with some cash in my pocket. I guess I'm real materialistic. It's important to me, but I'm not going to rob a bank or stand outside and grovel for it. I mean working and vacation, that's your whole life, right there.

It still makes me nuts when I'm out with my friends and joints keep getting flared up. I'm trying to stay away from it. But I do still get in fights. Just the other day I got in a fight with one of the guys I used to hang out with. He's a junkie and used to sleep in hallways. I've brought him to my house and fed him, and I gave him my own bed. But he wanted to fight me. First the cops broke us up, but we ended up fighting later. He ended up biting me. I didn't go out and start the fight—trouble just comes upon me.

People can think what they want. I don't care if they think I was in a gang. They think I'm going to be a loser and end up with seven kids and go on welfare. I know I'm going to get out of here. I don't want to stay in town or in the projects anymore. I want to get out, soon. Before I end up in jail or booting up.

Patrick has finished his GED and is attending a junior college.

II: LEAVING THE LIFE
How Kids Can Get out of Gangs

"It took me till I was about seventeen to acknowledge that Christ is the only way, that my boys aren't going to be there to get me out of situations."

—*Haywood, age 20*

"I was looking into my future and the consequences of what I had done. . . . I was like, God, please let me graduate."

—*Margie, age 18*

"I have to really pay attention to my daughter instead of the gangs. I have to take care of her instead of them."

—*Melissa, age 15*

"Nobody's willing to do anything. They talk about crime, but they never get active, and just counseling is not gonna help these guys. That's why I don't give up."

—*Daniel, age 22*

"You don't have to go and cure the world; just cure one kid. If you do something with that one kid, he or she may influence another."

—*Hewitt Joyner II, age 53*

Right now I'm trying to eat as much as I can from the Bible.... I read through Genesis to the ending of the book.... I carry around my date book, and I've put in it different verses dealing with anger, addiction—you know, just how to cope with different things in your life. I look through that during the day instead of going through the whole Bible. I grab those pieces of verses and think about them and work on them.

—Haywood Rogers, age 20

A godly man gives good advice, but a rebel is destroyed by lack of common sense.

A good man has firm footing, but a crook will slip and fall.

Hatred stirs old quarrels, but love overlooks insults.

Anyone willing to be corrected is on the pathway to life. Anyone refusing has lost his chance.

—Proverbs 10

For the reverence and fear of God are basic to all wisdom. Knowing God results in every other kind of understanding.

—Proverbs 9

FIVE

Walking with Christ

This chapter is dedicated to Haywood Rogers's father, Gary Stevenson.

Gang members are turning to places of worship for both a safe haven and a remedy for gang life. Some churches offer mentoring, family intervention, after-school tutoring, and parenting education. Many church-based programs follow the principles of twelve-step programs, treating gang involvement as an addiction, much like dependence on drugs or alcohol. In these programs, getting teens to leave their gang often requires admission of wrongdoing, faith in God, and the conviction to bring hope into their own lives and the lives of others.

Haywood Rogers, age twenty, lives in Roxbury, Massachusetts, with his grandmother. Since age nine, he has had help from Reverend Bruce Wall, a juvenile court clerk magistrate and a well-respected leader in the religious and African-American community in Boston. Still, Haywood became heavily involved in gangs until he was seventeen, when he became more active in his church. Like 50 percent of today's African-American children, Haywood was raised without a father in the home, and he speaks about the need in his life for a male role model. He also talks about replacing his faith in the gang with his faith in God.

Haywood Rogers

If I was going to say what helped me leave the life, I'd have to say, you know, that it was a lot of things. Getting out was gradual, and you have to have an alternative and be able to put your energy into something positive that's going to be in your best interest—as long as it's that and it's not the streets or something that can corrupt your mind or put you six feet under or behind bars. For me it's been walking with Christ.

It's also important to have a father figure, and for me that's been Reverend Bruce Wall. I've been going to his church off and on since the court put me there. Since I was little, he's always been there for me. He gives me a lot of hope. He still affects me all the time when he talks. I take a lot of things that he says to heart. I really do. It's like any other father who would challenge his son and say, "You have to stay on this path." It's not like he forces it upon you. It's like he lays them on the table and says, "Now choose." And even if I choose the wrong side, I know he's still there. And I can humble myself and say I made a mistake.

My parents split up before I reached the age of eight, and my pops wasn't home but he still came around. He was a pimp at one point. He hustled and

57

stole. I really had a family that was into the street life, and to me it was cool. You know if you grow up and your father and uncle are your role models, and that's what they do, you don't think it's wrong. You want to be like them.

Guys growing up without a father don't have that manly figure to teach them not to do this or how to respect a woman. I think some guys look at their mother as just a weaker part—like they can run over them. But they can't run over their father 'cause the father has that firmness, like, "You're not disrespecting me like that." They think, My mother is not going to have the answer—she's not going to understand what I'm going through. If they don't have their father to go home and talk to, they are going to find some other guy that's older. Some guys do look toward gangs for a family. Especially if kids grow up in the ghetto. They don't know what's on the outside.

I've been on the street since I was eight years old and basically doing what Haywood wanted to do, not listening to what my mom had to say. My mom and I never had a one-on-one conversation. It was more or less if I had a bad report card, I got a spanking. So when I was eight, I stole, I hustled, so I could have money in my pocket. I think my mom had pretty much an idea that most of my toys I stole. I mean I wasn't borrowing it from nobody's house. But I don't remember her saying too much, "You need to stop this." When I did go to school, it was mostly to beat up other kids. Even though I had the principal saying this is wrong, when I left and went home, there was nobody to say you are on punishment. I started smoking marijuana, getting into fights, telling teachers they could go and do whatever. Because I thought I was in charge.

Then came along my little sister, and I took care of her because my mom was on drugs. And my mom couldn't take care of my brother when he was born. He came up cocaine positive and premature, so he stayed at my grandmother's. At that time I got caught stealing a Michael Jackson doll for my sister. I got arrested and went to court and stuff. I was around nine. And that is when I met Bruce Wall.

I had to go before him. He worked at the magistrate clerk's office in juvenile court. I went with my mom, and he asked her to leave the room. He asked me if I wanted to be taken from my mother. And I said no. But I think in my mind, it was, Yeah, I do, because at home I could do anything I want.

In order for my case to be dismissed, I had to go to Bruce's church. So even then the court had put me in his care. He used to look out for me. Bruce even came one day and told the kids on the school bus not to mess with me or they'd have him

Haywood trying to help on the streets

to mess with. Around then I missed two or three months of school. Then the court took me away from my family and sent me to reform school. I didn't go for stealing, just 'cause my home situation wasn't functioning right. My whole home environment wasn't cool. My mom, you know, I wouldn't say was selling drugs, but she let people come to the house to use the drugs and charged them for that.

When I first got to reform school, I got in a lot of trouble just not wanting to listen to the staff. I had a real bad temper—anything could trigger me. I just didn't have no kind of discipline. I was free. I think the thing that was good about reform school was that I learned how to control my temper and how to really deal with things on the intellect level. I still saw Bruce, and he took me places on the weekends when I could leave school. He was there for me.

I got out of reform school at fourteen and went to an independent house. There were people that helped me there, but they didn't know exactly who I was with. I was hanging with the wrong crowd. I think I just wanted to be with the guys I felt comfortable with. So the first gang that came about, we patrolled the area, but we didn't carry weapons. You wouldn't just shoot somebody for the smallest thing, like over a girl. If anything you beat them up. You wouldn't go shoot innocent by-standers. I think the reasons for using the gun has changed, and the age. 'Cause you have eight-year-olds carrying guns. But if I had a chance to get hold of a gun at eight, I'd have had one.

When I got older, around fifteen or sixteen, I was really into gangs, and my family was in the life as well. Most of them hung with Castlegate. But I hung out with a variety of gangs. It was in Roxbury, Dorchester, Mattapan. 'Cause I knew Jamaicans, Haitians—I wasn't sticking with one crowd. But Humboldt was my home base. These were my boys and stuff. There were about twenty or thirty guys. Pretty much we would go out partying and get into beefs, you know, gang shootings, quarrels. I sold crack, stabbed people, got shot, shot people, and the whole nine.

We didn't think about shooting. You just do it. I find that a shame, that I had no morals about hurting somebody, that I could just go ahead and do it. You know it was nothing to me. It's like you done it so many times and seen it. When I did it, I didn't feel anything.

And selling drugs, I shouldn't have done it. I was killing off a race of people. You have a lot of people who are like, "Don't you feel bad that you sold crack?" But then I don't think I felt anything. When you sell crack, it's like you invest all your money into this, now you got to sell this so you can get more money and make your money back. If I had thought more about it, I would have changed it back then.

I still get depressed in the springtime because that's when a lot of my rela-tives got killed. Right after I got out of reform school, my cousin got shot by his own boy. He had a friend shoot him in his own home for drug money. And someone hit my uncle with a brick so they could take his money, and he died. And then my aunt got shot right outside her home for retaliation. Out of all of that going on, my family wanted to retaliate. I was like, "Man, I got to go and kill these people." But I didn't really want to. This was a truly hard time for me.

Then I realized that certain things in my life just wasn't right. I was a young teen that says, "How do I pull all those things together?" But things do pull together. That's when I started going to church more, meeting new people and doing different things. I had an alternative. And church gave me encouragement to go out there and fight the crime and stay focused on God. I love him. Because I can just go to him and talk to him. 'Cause after you do something wrong to somebody and you apologize, it's still on your conscience. So I ask him things to forgive me for. And know that I'm forgiven. I feel very at peace.

I thought about going back to the life about a year ago. I had a lot of unanswered questions in my head and was struggling with my walk with Christ. It was a hard decision to dislocate myself from the people that I was hanging with, and I miss the friendship. I had to push all these people out of my life, or I couldn't live the perfect Christian life. And dag, sometimes I wish I could see so-and-so. I also felt like there was security and it was always going to be there.

Even now I have friends that got my back. You know, I was scared less when I was in a gang. Now I do worry sometimes about being killed. I mean I could have enemies in the past that could still want to do harm to me. Now I always have to make sure I only have one shadow.

Haywood has found a new life in his church.

I think it was all about could I make it in the outer world. I said, I just can't give up that easily. It would really be a shame for me to slip and go all the way back, with all the things I had accomplished. I just kept saying, There are the things you need to do, like to actually give it back to the kids who are out there struggling. I kept turning back to God. It was like he pulled me out of this and pulled me out of that one. So then I felt he'll pull me through anything else in life.

So to keep my belief strong, I went to church, the Dorchester Temple Baptist Church. Bruce is copastor with Craig McMullen. Most Sundays I go, and we have singing. I love that part and the word getting in the Bible. Right now I'm trying to eat as much as I can from the Bible. When I wake up in the morning, I try to break open my Bible. I read through Genesis to the ending of the book. Sometimes I just try to memorize parts or put a star by them. I carry around my date book, and I've put in it different verses dealing with anger, addiction—you know, just how to cope with different things in your life. I look through that during the day instead of going through the whole Bible. I grab those pieces of verses and think about them and work on them.

During the week I work for Bruce Wall Ministries at the church. It's not just a thing I work for, because Bruce is like family to me. It is something positive, and it's something to reach out to the kids, and it's Christ-centered. It took a lot of planning and a lot of heart. And I feel 'cause I'm the younger generation I have to carry out Bruce Wall Ministries.

We have different programs. I'm a streetworker. If I see someone hanging out, I probably go up to him and talk to him about his life or about Christ. I see if I can persuade him to go somewhere and talk. I also go with Bruce into the community to have spiritual patrols, where we talk to the shop owners and stuff, just let them know that we want to do something about the gangs in our neighborhood. I love working with the kids at the church. A lot of them have problems, and I think I understand because I've been there. I learned how to survive on the streets, and I can relate when a kid says there is nothing out there for him, like, "My mother doesn't love me" or "I want to die today." I know where all that comes from because I know where all the hatred is coming from.

If you want kids to join the church, you have to learn how to accept them and interact with them without giving them only church stuff. They'll think it's being thrown at them, and they'll want to get out of there. If you have a person that comes from the streets, you can't just expect them to jump out of where they come from. It took me till I was about seventeen to acknowledge that Christ is the only way, that my boys aren't going to be there to get me out of situations. And when a kid comes into the church, and he's so used to tooling his gun and selling drugs, you can't expect him to leave all that stuff alone. He's got all the problems in the street he's dealing with, like family members dying, his boys dying. When he leaves the streets, he's going back to the ghetto and then the church is not with him. When he comes to the Sunday service, where's the support during the week? I want to help these kids.

But I realize I can't save everybody. You can only save the people that want to be saved. When you are working with a person, sometimes he's still in the life and he's telling you he's not. But you've been there and you know. So you try to pull him away from it. When he gets to a certain point and you feel stressed out, and you've got all these other kids you're trying to work with, you find yourself separating a little bit. They can call you and need you to help them, but at some point it is on them.

I help run a group called Gangs Anonymous. That's at our church on Thursday nights. At the meetings I deal with a lot of grown men in the face. And I'm not going to be the baby-sitter. They have to get up and walk. Right now I don't get so emotionally caught up in the thing that I can't function in my own life. If I do, I'll crawl up in my own hole, my own world, and I won't want to be bothered with everybody else. Sometimes I have to just take care of Haywood. Now I realize that all the stuff I see the kids putting me through, I already put someone else through— like Bruce.

Haywood talking at a Gangs Anonymous meeting with Bruce Wall

Bruce came up with the idea for Gangs Anonymous. I think he wanted to see if I could carry it, so I'd have that feeling of more leadership and be able to present things to our youth. He speaks at meetings, but he lets my friends Marcus and Bret run it with me. What we basically do is talk to guys about trying to stay out of the life. And if they haven't been in the life, we tell them where we came from so they won't want to get in. We're all male, and I think the youngest one that comes now is about ten years old. We invite leaders in the community, for role models, like one of the police superintendents. We talk about the feelings we have about family members and friends. We try to teach them how to communicate with one another without feeling less of a man. I see in some of the guys that they are struggling, trying to get away from the life. But when you get denied jobs and you get your hopes so high and then something crushes them hopes, you start to slide. I try to work with them on being able to try and move on and get hopes for something else.

Praying with Bruce Wall and other community leaders on a neighborhood Spiritual Walk

My favorite thing, I would say, is creating things to try to pull kids from the streets. When I'm not working at the church or studying, I teach kids rap and I choreograph dance for them so they have something positive to do. I'm pretty much the only one they talk to about their problems. I play a big brother role. I think that maybe I'm where I am now because of dance, too. I've been dancing since I was able to walk. Everywhere I went, I danced—on the streets, wherever. It was something I knew I had talent at. I used to perform and went on tour with a play once. Now I set up performances for the kids. I want to put a school in the center of Boston, like a dance or music school. But you don't need to qualify or know any kind of skill. Because you come in and we'll teach you that. Who knows, we might even have college courses. Kids say, "I got this talent, but where do I bring it and what can I do with it?" This would just give them a place to do it.

I'm pretty busy now taking care of a lot of things. I speak in public. I've done it many times. I say the best crowd to be talking to are kids that really don't have a clue on what's going on out there and are figuring out how to get out of their lifestyles. And adults that want to go into the community to help out. I spoke at the Peace Conference in Boston this summer about being in a gang. I think every time I speak, someone will get something out of it. Sometimes I get that certain stare from somebody, and I guess I said something good.

I also try to help out my family more. Before I wasn't in a place where I could help my sister, and now I check up on her. I see my mother whenever I get the time. She's a home care nurse now. But my father passed on about a month ago He was like forty-five years old and had AIDS. I never lost respect for him. I think I understood a lot of what he had to go through. Even when he was sick, we had good talks and he told me, "Don't ever give up. Stay on the right track."

Haywood teaches dance and rap to neighborhood kids.

Haywood in his church, happy he's "made it"

Just talking to him gave me a lot of motivation. You see the thing about it is we always had a relationship; it was just that he was never around. It's not like he can help certain situations or like my mother can help some. It's like there's no one to truly blame. If you keep blaming somebody and keep that hatred, when does it end? And when they die, it's too late to try to end it.

I know my father would want me to be strong now—not break down, so I can't focus on what I need to do. I want to try to stay in contact with my family and keep that family grip there. I mean, he always said he's proud of me. Once, when I really started hanging around him, he was at an NA [Narcotics Anonymous] meeting. Someone told me that he stood up and said I was one of the people that helped him out the most. He was so happy and proud that I was doing something positive. I know he's in a better place, because the week he passed, he had accepted Christ in his life. I feel like I know where he's at, and you know, he's at peace right now. And that's the greatest thing for me. But it's gonna be hard without him.

I had a social worker once that said to my mother I wasn't gonna amount to nothing, and I had certain teachers that said the same. And I made up my mind and said to one of them, "Are you stupid? Do you think I'm gonna be on the streets at the age of twenty-one?" I was like, "I'm not. I'm gonna have something there going for my life." And, you know I'm happy to say that I am going to turn twenty-one this year, and I'm even going for my diploma. Back when I was in the life, being dead wasn't really too much on my mind. Now if I die for doing something that I believe in, I guess it's God's will. But I've looked in the mirror and said, "I made it," and I'm not on the streets. I'm doing something with my life.

Haywood Rogers has received his high school diploma and is still working with Bruce Wall Ministries.

My Name

My name is a flower like it is a drink. I have never seen the flower, but my mother tells me it is a beautiful flower. I don't even know the color or if it comes in many different colors. I would like to see it one of these days to see its so-called beauty.

The drink I have seen and tasted. It comes in different flavors. The one I like the most is strawberry. Sometimes people make fun of my name and say, "Let's go have a Margarita." I don't think my name really fits my personality because my name is sweetness, gentleness, and full of bloom. I'm kind of the opposite. I'm not saying I'm mean or rough or tough. To some people that's who I am: "Chola Margie."

"She's mean," they'll say. "Don't mess with her—she'll kick your ass!" I mean, if people get to know me, I can be sweet and kind. But if their talk ticks me off, it's a whole different story. I don't think my name was meant for me, but the fact is, I'm stuck with it. It's all right because I don't use it much. I go by Margie, for short. I only use it when I want to impress a cute vato or a high society gente. Pero no todos saben que mi nombre es Margarita, la flor bonita y un trago muy sabroso.*

—Margarita Ledezma, age 18

chola: *barrio or gang kid;* vato: *guy;* gente: *person*
But not everybody knows that my name is Margarita, daisy, the pretty flower and the most delicious drink.

Mi nombre

Mi nombre es el de una flor al igual que de un trago. Nunca he visto la flor pero mi madre dice que es una flor hermosa. Ni siquiera sé su color o si viene en muchos colores. Me gustaría verla un día de estos y ver su tan mencionada hermosura.

El trago sí lo he visto y probado. Viene en diferentes sabores. El que más me gusta es el de fresa. A veces la gente bromea acerca de mi nombre diciendo: "Vamos a tomarnos una margarita." No creo que mi nombre caiga con mi personalidad porque significa dulzura, gentileza y floreciente. Yo soy algo contrario. No digo que sea mala, grosera o brusca. Para alguna gente eso es lo que soy: "Chola Margie."

"Ella es mala," dirán. "¡No la fastidies que te pegará!" Quiero decir que si la gente consigue conocerme, yo puedo ser dulce y amable. Pero si me provocan, es todo lo contrario. No creo que mi nombre sea hecho para mí, pero el hecho es que ese nombre me pusieron. Esta bien porque no lo uso mucho. Tengo mi Margie como sobrenombre. Solo lo uso cuando quiero impresionar un vato simpático o una gente de la alta sociedad. Pero no todos saben que mi nombre es Margarita, la flor bonita y un trago muy sabroso.

SIX

Looking into My Future

Wanting a better life motivates kids to leave gang life. Almost all of the teens in this book express this implicitly or explicitly in their interviews; they don't want to end up junkies or in jail or dead on the streets. They want to graduate from high school, support their families, or give back to their communities. As all of them would acknowledge, it is crucial to get out before it is too late. Or, as Saroeum Phoung says in chapter 2, "Don't wait until it's too, too deep. Like kill twenty people and go to jail and never get out."

Crimes tried in juvenile court are often gang-related. Convicted gang members under the age of eighteen obviously reduce their chances of ever finishing high school. Many experts believe that early intervention, treatment, and guidance are more effective than long-term incarceration, in part because of its negative impact on their education.

Margarita (Margie) Ledezma, eighteen, was born in San Jose, California, after her parents immigrated from Mexico. She joined a gang in her early teens and has been in jail several times. She left her gang because she wanted to finish high school. She enrolled at San Jose State University, an accomplishment she is proud of. With help from former gang member Tony Torres, who helps run the Gardner Teen Center, Margie also began working at the center, often with kids who are or have been in gangs.

Margie Ledezma

My family used to live in this house. Now I live here with my aunt, uncle, and two cousins. My mom left San Jose with my brother and little sister when I was about sixteen. She wanted to take me away from the gangs. She didn't realize that I wasn't going to go, 'cause I wanted to finish school and go to college here. So I stayed. My father, he moved back to Mexico when I was four. I think if he had been here, I would have ended up the same.

Some of the way I am, I got from my uncles who live next door, and two of them are closer to my age. They were bigger than me, so they'd throw and punch me around. I got in trouble for things they did. I just got mad and sick of it, so I figured I'm not gonna let no one fuck with me anymore. I guess I programmed myself to never be afraid of anybody, except for my mother. I have no idea why I'm afraid of her. But it's like this fear that I have if I do something, she's gonna know. But with everybody else, I'll take them on, big or small, fat or skinny. If I get my butt kicked, I get it kicked, but I'm not gonna back down. Guys don't really have to prove something, as opposed to women—they always have to prove that they're down. You know it's just the gender role

thing. But I see a lot of girls that are very wannabe people. To me, it's be yourself. I wasn't a wannabe or a gottabe; I just became.

The friends I hung around with at school, when I was fourteen, they were in a Brown Pride gang, you know, Chicano. You aren't really Norteño or Sureño, but both combined. But we really mostly had Norteño mentality inside, like to mess up Scraps [Sureños]. There were about fifty of us. Half were guys. There were tattoos involved and drinking, smoking pot, stuff like that. They chose me to be the leader because I could take a stand and I was able to take care of my business with a guy or a girl. They knew that I was pretty down. But it was on the far side of town, the north side, and I didn't really like going all the way over there. I wanted to be on my side. So I hung out with them for about a year, and then I just stayed here.

On the block where I live, my friend Christine and I are the only girls. Except for her, all my friends are guys. So, before I got into the first gang, the guys here on the west side already knew me. So when I joined the gang over here, they told me, "We're not going to jump you in because you'll probably kick one of our asses." I said, "If you guys want, I'll take six of you. I have no problem with it." And they're like, "Oh, no, kick back, you crazy girl." So we left it at that. The gang over here was like a lot of generations. In my generation there was about forty, mostly guys. My name was the one the first gang gave me, La Payasa [The Clown], because all I did was make people laugh. I'd talk dirty or make stupid faces, and they'd just crack up. I was funny, but then I was also crazy and I was rough.

I think the good part of gangs is if you can't find something at home or if you don't get appreciated, or love, then you get it in the gang, because they give you respect. They're happy, as opposed to a broken-down family, like the way I was. Then there's the bad part, which was going out and causing trouble and killing people. What makes me upset about gangs is you are going to lose people, regardless—innocent people, enemies, or friends. Like my friend was shot in the head by a Sureño. She wasn't in a gang. She was just in a bad place at a wrong time and with people affiliated with Norteños. She was about to get married. She was seven months pregnant. When she died, I was upset, and man, it made me pissed.

Another thing that gets me mad is how they stereotype gangs in the media. They say any organization that has two or three people is considered a gang. They always look at youngsters and their gangs and all. But the way I look at

Margie with her friend Christine

it, the government's like this big ol' gang. They're basically controlling people. And it drafts people for the war. And that's killing people, because some of them are going to die. Think about it—is that a gang?

There's all kinds of gangs, not just Mexican kids. There's white gangs, black gangs, Filipino gangs, Chinese gangs. But the ones people look at the most are the Chicano gangs. The ones on TV are hard-core—they just don't care, and they're throwing their sign. Not all gangs are like that. The media tends to come around when there's violence, like when there's a shooting. They don't take the time to come and see what we're capable of. And a lot of my friends are intelligent and they can draw beautiful art and write poetry. They think we're all stupid and all we do is fight and kill people.

Fighting is not always necessary, but it's been the only way I can handle things sometimes. I was never going out to just shoot people or anything. And after a fight, I feel bad for what I had done to that person.

The first time I got arrested, I was around fifteen. It was for a concealed weapon on a school campus. Some girl had a knife in her purse, and there were narcs rushing her, so she thought they were going to check her. She said, "Here, hold my purse." I said fine. I didn't know there was a fatal machete in there. Then one cop said, "What do you have in there?" And I said, "I don't know, officer. This isn't mine." He snatched it away and threw it, and this big knife came out, and I'm going, damn. The girl was afraid to be in jail by herself, so she said I knew the knife was in there. So I got busted also. She really messed me over. The thing that got me even more was that she got out before I did. She said, "I'll write you," and I'm like, fuck you. I was in for a couple of days—juvenile hall.

They put me in a cell by myself. They have a unit for girls, and the other ones are for guys. They gave me clothes, a toothbrush, blankets and made me take a shower. It was gross in a way, 'cause you had to wear their bras and their underwear. I was like, Damn, I can't believe I'm in here. I used to talk shit about how can people be in jail, and here I'm in jail myself. I wasn't really claiming at the time, but I was wearing red. They said, "Do you claim?" And I said no. They said, "Why are you wearing all red?" I go, "Just because I wear certain clothes doesn't mean that I claim it." I was like, Fuck you—I'm not. I was nothing at the time. I was just starting to get into that stuff.

That was the first time. By the second and third time I got arrested, I was already into gangs. I got in fights and was arrested for assault and battery. I was in jail for about a week. My mom drove down to come and get me out. She wasn't really mad, just disappointed. I never got convicted, but my charges are on file, two felonies. So I got a diversion, where they put you on probation, and I had a probation officer for almost a year. Then about a year ago, I got busted for possession of a deadly weapon.

It was my mother's ice pick that she had, just in case, for protection. I didn't want her to one day use it on somebody. So I put it in this purse that I never use. Then one day I went to work and just threw my stuff in it. I was walking and saw some of the guys. I went to go buy beer, and we were in the park drinking. I put the extra beer in my bag, and then we got caught by rookie cops. They were all crazy, like they were FBIs. They started searching me. When one of them took my purse, he didn't ask me for information, so I knew he was a rookie. He pulled out the ice pick, and I hadn't even remembered it was in there. They thought it was the guys'. They didn't think I would have one. I said, "No, it's mine. I forgot it was in there, and I'm sorry." Then I tried to make up this long excuse, that I've got to walk from work and I carry it for protection. They didn't fall for it.

They took me in to an investigations bureau to see if I had any meat on me, information about the gang. I thought, Oh, shit, they're going to squeeze me. They handcuffed me to the table and said, "If you don't talk, you can do a maximum of three years for an illegal weapon." They'd ask me hard-core stuff like, "Where are the drugs? Where are the guns?" God knows, I knew all kinds of stuff. But, I'm like, "I don't know." I might have known, but that's something I couldn't say 'cause I'd be jeopardizing my life. If the other guys would have found out, that's considered snitching. So basically I told them typical stuff they already knew, like where we hang out. They thought by scaring me, they'd get something out of it, but they didn't.

I got out the same night. The cops hadn't asked me permission to see my bag, and they didn't read me my rights until later. So it was an illegal search, and I never got charged. But they have my picture and my fingerprints. I had already been in jail before, so I wasn't really scared, more worried. Sitting there all those hours, all I could think of was I hope they let me graduate. I was looking into my future and the consequence of what I had done. That's all I was worried about. I was like, God, please let me graduate. And then I'll do as many years as they want to give me.

When I saw everything come down in jail, that's what really got me out of the gang. But before that, it's unbelievable how I had the time to do homework and still have time to do what people call gang-bang. I had this teacher who knew I was in a gang. He would say, "*Chola* Margie, I can't believe how smart you are." He was one of my favorite teachers for English, creative writing. He really helped motivate me. He totally had faith in me and said, "I know you're going to be a writer one of these days. Your poetry is beautiful." That would make me feel good.

During this time, I started to work at the Gardner Youth Center. I went there because it's in my neighborhood. The guy who helps run it, Tony, he used to be in a gang. And he was like a dad 'cause he took care of me. He'd say, Margie, you need to do this and that. He knew I lived around here and these are my people, and I was gonna hang out with them. But he saw in me that I was good in school and that I shouldn't be in a gang. Tony lets me know when I do good and when I mess up. He's cool with me, and I'm cool with him. I'm really glad

Margie teaching boxing at the Gardner Teen Center

that I hooked up with him. I guess he saw what I was capable of, because he helped get me a contract with the city to work at Gardner. First I worked part-time and now permanently.

The center helps kids, and it's great because it's open late hours and they're creating new programs so there are more things to do. I'm a recreational aide. I work with the kids, and I help Rudy teach boxing. I started learning about two years ago. I got in a fight with this girl, and she popped me real good in the eye and gave me a shiner. I popped her back, and when I couldn't get her off of me, I thought, Man, I got to do something. No one in my life had ever given me a shiner, guy or girl. I told Rudy about it, and he said come on in. So that's when I started to get into boxing.

Now when I get pissed, I try to talk to people. Or when I get in one of those moods, like when my friend got shot, I write. I kinda just figured it out. I started writing just one day when I was at another job. When people would say something that got me angry, I'd write a poem and think about it. I started to write in high school, but now I have a class in college where I write poems and essays.

The greatest thing for me was to see if I could get into San Jose State. It would have been like small town to me, to go to the city college, because anybody can get into junior college. People want to say I'm this *cholo* type. I wanted to prove that even people like me can get into the big house. At first I didn't get accepted 'cause they thought I was missing all these years, but I wasn't. They just hadn't seen all my transcripts. I knew I should have been accepted, so I didn't worry. I went over there for an interview, which was gonna be an appeal, but they said, "Oh, we made a mistake. We're truly sorry—you should have been accepted the first time." So I was like, I did it! I'm the first person to go to college in my family, but they don't really have the knowledge of what being in college is about. Of course they were proud when I got accepted.

With some guys from the center

I work on the weekends and study, and I go to visit my mom or she comes here. You know, I miss my mother now. It's weird, but I miss her yelling at me. But this weekend she was peaceful, and I kinda liked it. I guess sometimes she knows I've changed, but she doesn't want to see it and that I've grown up. I guess I understand now that she worried about all the things that go on in society with the gangs, the rape, the drugs, and jail. She had all that in her mind. See, she always told me, "I worry about you—you're my daughter." But when I was younger, I didn't see what she saw. And now she finally realized I am eighteen. I'm not saying I'm a full adult yet. But I could pretty much take care of myself. And I told her if anything is wrong with me, I'll let her know. I'm not going to hide nothing from her.

If I have kids, I'll tell them I was in a gang. I would tell them the good and the bad about it. I think if I always converse with them—"How's school?"— and go toward the school things, then maybe they won't go that route. I'd want them to know about their culture and speak Spanish. I think it has more meaning than the English language, like when there's a real strong meaning in Spanish that you can't explain in English. I really want to have a career or graduate with a degree before I have kids. I don't want my kids to live poor or where I gotta go to welfare. That's something that's X'ed out right there. And if I had a kid now, that's something I would have to do. And if I was to get married, I'm not gonna be at home barefoot, washing dishes. I want the guy to be equal to me.

I learned that whenever there's situations, you gotta look at it from every direction to know where people are really coming from, like working with the kids at Gardner. There's a lot of people out there that might get called *cholo* and have this fierce image, but inside it can be the most beautiful person, and that's what people don't take time to look at. They just call us gang bangers. If you want this world to get better, that's not the way to go. You gotta put yourself in our shoes. Just picture yourself without your dad or mom because they're always at work. You really then don't have nothing but school and friends. So because I was in a gang or 'cause of where I live doesn't mean that I'm a bad person. You know, I tell my little cousins that not all *cholos* and *cholas* are bad. I tell them they're just people like you and I and that Chicanos are in between Mexicans and Americans. Neither wants them, so they have their own culture, their own *Chicanismo*. People gotta be able to understand the differences within our society. Just like if you go over to Willow Glen, you see the little town

Taking care of her cousins

houses, they're all clean-cut as compared to ones around here—they're all broken down. But just because they're like that doesn't mean there's not beautiful people inside that house.

In some ways I'm not really staying away from the gang, because I live here, so I can't really get away from it. You just grow out of it. Because once you start getting educated, you're going to change. You become very athletic, or academics kind of pulls you away. You have to be on top of things, and you don't have time to kick back. And then you have a better chance of getting a good

Margie knows now that she has inner strength to draw on.

job. If I didn't have what I do now, school and work and all, I probably would end up being with them. I guess I'm proud the gang is still a part of me and I'm a part of them. If anything was to happen to me, they'd still go out of their way to be there for me, and if anything was to happen to them, I'd help them. But I have to be careful because if I get arrested again, I've got three felony arrests. But I can't really get in trouble unless I fight, and I'm not going to fight. It does always cross my mind that I might be in the wrong place. So if the guys talk about going to do something I'm like, "Good-bye, I'll see you later."

I think what I like to do the best at Gardner is to stop these guys who were in gangs from doing things. I tell them to think about what they're doing first. When I graduate, I know I want to do something that helps people, like be a social worker or a counselor or even a probation officer. I want people to know that even though I was in a gang, I have knowledge about things and I made it to college. That way stereotypes of Mexicans or Chicanos, that they only work at McDonald's or pick in the fields, will slowly go away.

I think a lot of Chicanos have a lot of dreams. They don't get to 'em because of the streets. And I'm proud of myself because, you know, I was like a tree. This tree was growing up straight, and then I just started getting in the teen years, bending and going the other way. And when the tree was like that, everybody wanted to break down the tree. But the tree was too strong. Like those really tall California redwood trees. Except that in my case my tree has little dents and curves. It's always going to have them because those are the experiences in life that I have. Whether they're good or bad experiences, I like to put them away as a lesson. That way I can learn more and be prepared. To me it's not like life's a game but just a series of obstacles that you gotta go through. And then when you get over them, that tree starts growing straight again.

Margie has taken a leave of absence from school to work as a full-time recreational leader at Gardner Teen Center. She still hopes to graduate from college.

Strong Like a Boulder

I am built strong like a boulder;
my barrier will never break.
People won't know what's inside
and I can give life all it takes.
Truly I am noticed like a blossom in the weeds;
I stand out, and I'm different by all means.
My brain is like a plant inbred safely in its
roots;
I cannot be a flower because I'm firm like a
fruit.

I am like a butterfly contained to my cocoon.
Waiting to show how beautiful I am, soon.
I am like a flag.
Alone I stand.
Proud of what I do.
Proud of who I am

—Tanika Crockett, age 16, Riverside High School, Buffalo, New York

SEVEN

For My Daughter

Leaving a gang is rarely easy or accepted by fellow gang members, who consider it to be like breaking family loyalty. The rules to get out can be harsh. Not only are kids beaten up by other gang members, but they also can be shot or even killed. When a member leaves because of pregnancy and parenthood, though, her departure is usually both safe and sanctioned. Surprisingly or not, gangs respect both the need to have a family and the responsibilities that go with it.

Becoming a parent can motivate members to leave, in hope of finding a better life for their child than the streets can provide. As Saroeum Phoung says in chapter 2, "I guess the kid really pulled me out from the street. I was feeling like any fool can make a baby, but it takes a real man to raise a child."

Because it is common for gang members to have sex, girls in gangs are part of the over one million teenagers in the United States who become pregnant each year. Besides having sex once in a gang, some girls choose to be "sexed in" to join. Sometimes this includes being told to have unprotected sex with multiple gang members. Since gang members often come from fragmented families, they may strive to create balanced families of their own. However, many girls raise their children alone: One half of children under six who are born to girls younger than eighteen live with one parent only.

Fifteen-year-old Melissa Sabater lives with her mother and almost two-year-old daughter in the Mission Hill projects in Boston, Massachusetts. At thirteen she joined a gang, then later became pregnant by a rival gang member. Melissa believes that nearly all of the girl members left her gang because they became mothers. Streetworkers, a gang intervention program described in chapter 9, helped Melissa stay out of the gang after having her daughter.

Melissa Sabater

I'm not in GOYA gang anymore. GOYA stands for Gun On Your Ass. It was like forty girls and forty guys. We hung out in the Mission Hill projects, where I live with my mother. My parents are from Puerto Rico. My dad lives in Boston, but I don't know exactly where. He wasn't around at all when I was growing up. I have two sisters and only two brothers now because my brother Carlos died of an overdose of drugs—crack cocaine—when he was twenty-seven. He was the one I was closest to. My sister Carmen has HIV. She's eighteen and five months pregnant. My sister who lives in Charlestown is twenty-six and has two kids. Edgar is twenty-three and is in Puerto Rico because he used drugs, so my mother sent him back there. Greg is twenty and is all fine.

I joined GOYA when I was thirteen. I had been hanging out since I was little. Carmen and Greg was in it so I was, like, If they are in it, then I could be in it,

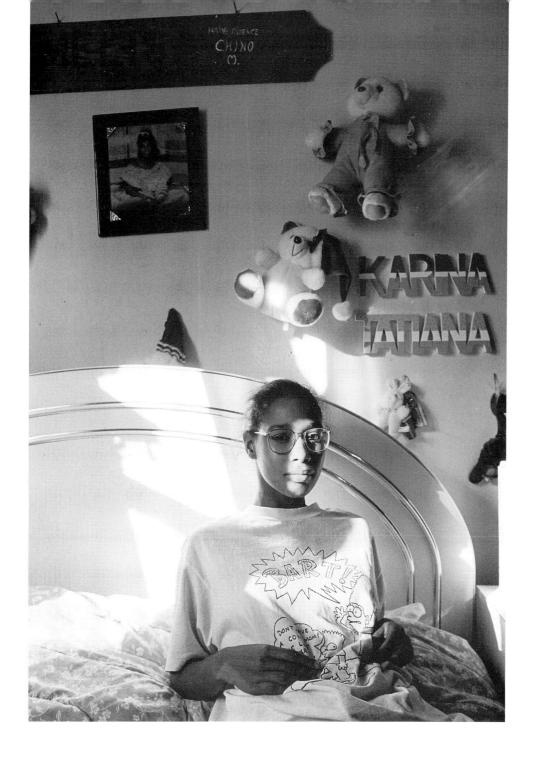

too. So I just joined them. But they told me I couldn't do the things they do. They watched out for me. If we was going to get shot up, they be like, "Duck, Melissa, or they gonna shoot you." So I be ducking. One day they brought this girl over, and they wanted me to fight her. So I did it, and I won. That's how I joined. I was the youngest in the gang. I was the baby.

GOYA, we were a family. We would all get together, and if anyone needs help, they there for us. You know, it's like we give them love, they give us love. We give them respect, they give us respect. We all care. You want to get out, you know, that's their business. We ain't gonna be like, "No, you ain't getting out before I kill you."

We would hang out and smoke herbs and drink, have a little party. For me I was young and was having mad fun. We usually steal cars or jump somebody, take their money and whatever they have. I liked what they were doing, shooting other gangs. They was like, "Melissa, you can't do it" so I was like, "I want to do it. I want to try and see how it feels." So once we went in a car by Mozart, a rival, Mozart Park Boys, and started bucking at them. I feel proud of myself when I used a gun. I didn't hit anybody. But I was like, Wow, I did it. I am happy.

My moms didn't know I had a gun, but my sister and brother knew, and they carried one, too. I don't have it no more. I sold it to somebody that needed it really bad. But I still got the bullets. I'm just holding them—I don't know why, to remember, I guess. I would be nervous now if saw someone with a gun. Now I'm scared of guns.

There is a lot of drug dealing and baseheads around here. They use whatever drugs they can get, like crack, cocaine, diesel. My point is that they are in the gang because they need a job. You need a GED or a diploma to get a job. This is what all of these kids want, a job so they can get out of here.

In GOYA we didn't do the drugs except smoke weed. We only used to sell. Down this street near my house there's a block, and we used to hang down there and sell. I felt good because I needed money. Other people would get it and give it to us, and we'd sell it. I would make $150, give them a hundred and keep fifty, save it on my daughter. I wouldn't do it again if I find work. But if I don't get a job, then I'll do it again 'cause I need that money for my daughter.

Karina, my daughter, she's the reason I got out of GOYA. She is about one years old now. I was involved in the gang until I had her. When I was fourteen, I got pregnant from somebody in a gang we hated. They're all Puerto Ricans, Hondurans, Ecuadorans. Chino—that's Karina's father—is Honduran. I was

Melissa with her daughter, Karina

with him when I wasn't getting along with my boyfriend Eric. I've been going out with Eric for four years. He is good and not into gangs or anything. He's the type that don't like to fight. He's in a private school and just plays basketball after school. On that day that I slept with Chino, it just happened, you know, it just happened.

I found out I was pregnant when they made me a physical checkup at my after-school program. I had been going to it since I was a little girl. Ever since they told me I was pregnant, I was crying and crying all day for nine months because when I told Chino I was pregnant, he denied it was his. I told him it was, 100 percent. But he kept on telling me it wasn't and his moms kept on telling me it just wasn't his.

Then I got accepted to a school for pregnant girls in junior high. My social worker from DSS [Department of Social Services] told me about it. I had a social worker because when I was in the gang, I used to run away and not come back like for a week or two months. So my mother called DSS, and I was in their custody.

We did everything at that school. They give you vitamins and breakfast and lunch. Everything is free over there. And before, at my other school, I don't eat 'cause I don't have no money. I had to go to a clinic for my checkups. My preg-

With her mom and daughter

nancy was OK except for getting sick in the morning. Everything I'd eat, I would throw it up.

The guys in GOYA took care of me when I was pregnant. I'd be hungry, so they used to take me places every time I'd complain. Everybody in the gang tells you not to do drugs when you're pregnant. So I only smoked weed once. If I had done the other, crack, diesel, they would really get mad at us and tell us, "Don't do this, 'cause it's bad. Please don't do it, 'cause we don't want to see you die."

It was kind of hard when I had Karina. But I stood there strong. I had medicine in the back, and they told me it was going to hurt afterward, and it still does. My mom helped me a lot when I had her. It didn't take me that long to, like, change her diaper because my mother was there and then I knew how to do it. My mother had custody of Karina then, but now I do.

I'm proud of myself that I have Karina and am out of it. One reason is because of Hewitt. I don't know what would happen if he weren't here. He was the one that talked me out of it. He was at my school, at Southie [South Boston High School], hanging out, talking to everybody. And

A supportive hug from Hewitt

some people told me about him, that he's good at helping. Everybody used to go to his office so I was like, wow, let me go, too. He introduced himself and said he works at Streetworkers and helps people out. So I told him I had a baby and I didn't want to go to school, and he was like, "Nah, go to school." He talked me out of being in the gang and said, "It's not good for you. You have a daughter now." And you know, I was thinking, if I still be in the gang, DSS is gonna take my daughter away, and I don't want that to happen.

I talk to Hewitt every day in school, and he always calls me so we can talk

Melissa can confide in Hewitt.

about my problems, and he helps me with them. Because my family, we don't talk about everything, like my sister having HIV. She don't like talking about it. She got it from her ex-boyfriend, who died of it. She didn't know nothing. Or I talk to him about my brother who died. I can't imagine that someone would give me that good advice, like about my daughter and my family. I'm real happy that I got a person just like that.

I try to keep on hanging on, you know, but it's hard to have a baby. When Karina gets me mad, I just breathe in and out a couple of times. That's it—I just count. If she just keeps doing something that makes me mad, I don't be banging her. It's easier now because at the beginning, she was just crying and crying, and I'm like, What you want? Oh, my God, give her the bottle—she don't want the bottle. The pacifier, give her that. And now it's easy 'cause she will point and take you where she wants. My mother takes care of Karina during the day when I go to school and sometimes my brother and sister help out.

It's hard to not be able to hang out with the gang. Now everybody went separate because they got babies. Sometimes I miss this and that about the gang. My sister does, too. When she be lonely in her room sometimes, we'll get together and talk about it. We say we should all get together again and have a party. They all still talk to me because we still in the gang. Because it is like the gang is in our heart. If we got any problems, we could just call them and go solve it. We don't shoot no more, we don't stab no more, but if another gang come and stab us, then we will do the same thing to them back.

I am kind of happy that I'm out of it, because I have to really pay attention to my daughter instead of the gangs. I have to take care of her instead of them. My daughter goes first and then them. No matter what, if I be in the gang now, I could get killed now or tomorrow. I want to get out of here because these parts ain't good for me and my daughter. Anybody could run by and just start shooting at us.

I don't want my daughter to know what I did in a gang. She could be like, oh, my mother did it, then I could do it, too. I don't want her to do the same thing as me, 'cause then one of the other gangs could kill her. I don't want that to happen to my daughter. I don't want her to know how to use a gun. If I saw her use drugs or a gun, I'll put her in DSS and lock her up.

I take Karina to see Chino in jail. He's been there, on and off, since he's thirteen. Now he's eighteen and in because they caught him with a stolen weapon twice. They caught him with drugs, and they're accusing him of killing a girl who was pregnant and a guy. But I don't know. 'Cause he don't be telling me everything. I wish he hadn't done it, but that's his business. I can't do nothing about it. I can't bring them back to life. When I was with him he got out on leave from DYS [Department of Youth Services]. He never even saw me pregnant. Then I went over to visit him when I got out of the hospital. And when he saw my daughter, he was shocked. He was like staring at my daughter, like, wow, it's mine. Now, every time we go to see him, we sit down on a table upstairs, and we wait and wait, and then when he comes, Karina goes and runs to him. We always write. And I miss him.

I really care about Eric, too. I love him. He knows I was in the gang, and he tries to help me. He was like, "Don't do this; don't do that." But if Chino got out of jail, I'd have to quit Eric. It would be hard. It would take a real while to forget about him. But there's a lot of girls out there that don't got a father. I don't want that to happen to my daughter. When my daughter grows up, then she's going to be like, "That's not my father," and I don't want her to say that. I want Karina to know her father.

My family is closer now. We stick together and go places together. I even see my father. It's like I got my daughter now, so he calls me and tells me he wants me to go over there with her. So I go visit him. I also wish for my sister to get better. I pray for her and for my daughter's father, every night. I wish we could all be back together—Chino, Karina, and me. I wish we could be part of a family.

I'm doing well in school now. It is going fine, really great. I want a good home. I want to finish school and go to college. I want to be a secretary, because I like to type—or a teacher. I would teach math. It don't matter what kind of people, black, white, Puerto Rican—it don't matter. Just me and my daughter, I want to have a good life, and that's it. I don't want to get married unless that person would treat me right and take care of my daughter, too.

My special dream, if I could have one, would be I want my daughter to go to

Melissa and her sister Carmen playing with Karina

Coming out of her home in Mission Hill

school, graduate, go to college, and have a good career. Not a bad one like me. I don't want her to just drop out and do nothing. When she grows up, she'll know the good things, not the bad things, and she won't get pregnant or be in a gang. I want good for my daughter, not bad.

Melissa is now in the Job Corps outside of Boston, a national federally funded residential program that helps kids finish high school, go to college, or enroll in vocational school. Melissa is studying for her certificate to become a paralegal. Her mother takes care of Karina.

COAST WEEKLY

FREE

January 6-12, 1994

LOCAL HEROES '94

Gunshots terrorize Sherwood

By Ricky de la Torre
The Californian

A quiet afternoon ended in terror Sunday for Sherwood Park visitors when gunfire erupted between rival gangs during a football game to promote peace.

The shooting started a melee that sent players, spectators and picnickers running for cover. It left a 14-year-old boy with a stab wound ____ and a head gash, police ____

PUBLIC FORUM

ot Just Fun and Games

s League needs your help. BY DANIEL VILLEG

nas Valley Sports League
) is a program that ___
ung men ___
ited to pl ___
rs are gan ___
bers. Som ___
play spor ___
zed sport ___
L by talk ___
Salinas. ___
ut they n ___
ar of talk ___
trying to ___
cies to h ___
d playing ___
ortunatel ___
there we ___

The Salinas Valley

BY BOLBOL

Leaders plan to re-examine football league

SVSL can be what-ever the community needs it to be, but it will depend on you.

JE would like to

Local Heroes

Coast Weekly salutes five men and ...

Local football league plays

By Christy Ne...

The Californian

The cloc...
sports pro...
Salinas ...
membe...
altern...
viole...

T...

volunteers,'' Villegas said. ''We
had enough players and they ...
had fun, but it takes more...

Bolbol said she ...
trouble ...

The Californian

City officials feared vio...
would break out after crea...
the new community...
league, Mayor Alan S...
Sunday.

After Sunday's sh...
munity leaders vow...
the league and ...
should help it ...
its own.

The city ...
league be...
tured, Styl...

''It's

stop the violence, now

the violence and said th...

... to say enough is

...y salutes five men and women for their efforts to better the communit...

ere...
the foot...
Villegas...

# of a sudden, we heard gunshots

...n Villegas of Salinas

unnecessary roughness. P...s are forbidden, but no fouls a...
luckily there were only three injuries for the season, whic...
ended this week. The league remains uninsure...

Villegas believes the league's success is evidenced by
the change of attitude that occurred by the end...
season.

''During the f...

EIGHT

Off the Streets

Having something else to do other than hang out on the streets can help kids avoid gang life. Whether it is learning to dance and rap, as Haywood Rogers talks about in chapter 5, boxing as Margie Ledezma describes in chapter 6, or a night basketball program such as the Peace League, mentioned in chapter 9, intervention programs use activities to build discipline, confidence, and communication. Employing former gang members as the coaches, mentors, and instructors in such programs, as is done in Gangs Anonymous and the football team discussed below, has proven to be especially effective for kids at risk.

Daniel Villegas, twenty-two, was born in Mexico and lives in Salinas, California. At thirteen, largely because all of his six older brothers and sisters were involved in gangs, he joined a Mexican-American Sureño gang. Strong family bonds and pride in a Mexican heritage have always been an essential element of Mexican gangs, which began in California as early as the 1920s and 1930s.

In Salinas, homicides have tripled in the last ten years, and the majority of violent crimes are committed by gang members. When the city requested community suggestions to combat gang violence, Dan submitted a proposal to create a football league for rival gang members. He received funding from the city, provided by the federal Housing and Urban Development Department. The league grew to include 180 teenagers. As well as working with the league, Dan enrolled in the criminal justice program at Hartnell College. He is one of the growing number of ex–gang members who are dedicated to helping others leave gang life.

Daniel Villegas

My father brought my family to the United States from Mexicali, Mexico, so he could work over here in the lettuce fields. We've all worked in the fields, my brothers and sisters and my mother. My father was really strict, big time. He would never let us go out or anything. He was an alcoholic, and mean, and there was a lot of physical abuse. We were being supported by him, and he left us. Then, I mean, everything collapsed. But my mom taught us that we had to be united, like a lot of Mexican families. There would be struggles, sacrifices, but as long as we stayed together, we would accomplish something. She taught us to be religious and what's right and wrong, like to respect other races, because we were discriminated against. We've always had good values, but not big values because we've had poverty. But my father was still missing in our lives. My mom had to work in the fields, so she wasn't around as much. We were all by ourselves.

My oldest brother, Victor, was like a father figure to me growing up. All my brothers were, because after my dad left, they took responsibilities for him.

They had to work, usually in the fields, to support our family and go to school, too. But they also wanted to have enjoyment. They needed to do something to relieve themselves. So my brothers started to get into gangs. I guess they wanted to try what they couldn't do when my dad was around. And they sort of got out of hand.

A gang has things in common, and they dare to do crazy things, like break the law, of course. They trust each other. It's like a second family, and if your first family doesn't listen to you, the gang will. In a gang—and again I'm going to compare it to a family—there's the shot callers. It's like a father and mother who'll tell one of the young ones, "Go to the store" or "Do a drive-by." And whoever listens, they'll be more caring to that kid and respect them more. Kids listen to *veteranos*, veterans.

Here gangs weren't much about drugs—it's more about neighborhoods and pride. My brothers and I, we have our Mexican pride. The gang can be your identity, and it's cultural. Back then the Norteño gangs, Chicanos who were born here and knew more English and less Spanish, put my brothers aside because they didn't speak English and were born in Mexico. So my brothers joined a Sureño gang. Victor and Ramiro were MBL'ers [Madeira Barrio Locos]. Madeira is the street we lived on. And it's still a gang. My brother Chuey was in the Vagos, another thirteener [Sureño] gang. My sisters Juana and Rosa hung out with guys from MBL and were sort of in the gang, too.

I was about ten when my brothers and sisters were partying and getting into trouble. They used to dress me up, the way the gang dressed—like ironing three marks in their shirts. They took me to parties, and I always enjoyed being with them. I watched the fights, but I never feared for myself. I guess I thought, Why are they gonna hit me? I'm small. When I would see a knife or a gun, I wouldn't be scared because I'd think, Well, maybe everybody has 'em. So when I held one, I didn't think, this is bad or this ain't right. And whatever I learned, I took it to school. In about fourth grade I brought a small knife to school to fight some of the guys. I never thought, this is wrong, because I was always around it.

When I joined a gang, around thirteen, I did it mostly because I saw my brothers being involved. At the time, my brothers and my mom were working a lot. My older sister took care of me, but pretty soon I would come from school and go with my friends until ten P.M. I started to hang out in a gang on Madeira Avenue. There were only about twenty-four of us, the Barrio Boys. We smoked weed and had beer runs—you steal beer and run out. There were a lot of Norteño gangs we always had conflict with. Usually it was at *quinceñeras* on the weekend. We would fight them with sticks, knives, and punching. We also used guns, so there were stabbings and shootings.

When you're the assassin and you harm someone who is the victim, at the time you're not supposed to feel any sympathy. Gang members are supposed to be bad and cool. When you're strong, you're not supposed to think about what you did to others. You think, Well, it could have been worse if it was me, my sister, or someone I know. Back then, my friends and I did a lot of stupid things.

Dan and his brothers Victor and Chuey barbecuing dinner for their family

I had friends who got killed, and going to the burials, I thought, What does this mean? Now I think a lot more about the family. I think, What would my mom say if I got caught or if she got shot? It was totally opposite of what she taught me. Or, like my cousin, who was in prison for four years. He helped me visualize what it would be like. What he told me did scare me. And my brother Chuey, he was always the troublemaker, and a lot of guys would respect him from his group. So what worried me was a gang incident when they hit him really bad. They almost, well, they opened his head, and you couldn't even tell who he was. And my mom also freaked out—she was scared big time.

By about sixteen or seventeen, I was getting out of gangs, but I was still partying and missing a lot of my classes. My grades were dropping, and they dropped me out of high school. I started at continuation school, and when I was there, I didn't care about school. Everybody was always playing around, and the teacher didn't care what we learned. There were a lot of gang members and pregnant girls and I thought, This isn't like high school. I said I am never going to learn like this. So I started studying and studying. I got enough credits to transfer back to high school, and I was happy I got out of there. I had more confidence, and I graduated from high school.

By then my gang sort of broke up. We spread out little by little, but some of the guys are still in gangs. I think they had a different family from me. I mean that's where it all starts. I believe my family gives me advice because they don't want me to go through what they did. My brothers wouldn't like to see me shot. And since I'm the youngest in the family, they want me to do something better, not work in the fields or hang around in the streets. They've gone through struggle and sacrifice, coming to this country to work in the fields. And it sort of takes generations, and now it's up to me to do the next step, to go to college, and make better of ourselves. What is good for me will help my family. Like my mom, I want to be able to buy her a house. She's everything to me. You know, I'll die for my mom.

I've always loved to play football. It's where I got a lot of respect. Guys would tell me, "I saw you playing football, and you're fucking bad." I'm not bragging—it's what they told me. There would always be guys playing from rival gangs. I still bad-mouthed everybody on the field, but afterwards, I saw we were all fine. Then they would ask me to play with them later. It's not just the playing, but it's when we're finished and we go to a party or see people out on the street, like a Norteño I had been playing with. They'd look a lot more hard-core at a party.

But now we could say, *"Hora le pues"*—Hey there, remember me? I never expected to get along with them, but you do because you remember playing with them.

This gave me the idea for the Salinas Valley Football League. I started arranging games around three years ago, but it was unstructured. I wanted to set up games with the rivals. We'd just play, and it started to work out of no-where, when it was unexpected. Then the police department put in the paper that they wanted some opinions for citizens concerned about violence, and that encouraged me to make the games structured.

When I first told the police chief about my idea, he didn't take me serious. He said it was gonna start fights and someone was gonna get shot. He said it was too much of a risk. But maybe it would work later on. He really got me believing that this can't work. The city wanted to concentrate on young kids, on the wannabes. And I absolutely dis-agree. We do need to help kids out of a gang at an early age, but in Salinas, you have to help the older ones. In reality, the young ones are gonna step out in the sidewalks and look up to older gang mem-bers. They're the ones in control and recruiting young kids.

Dan at Salinas Valley Football League practice

About a year later, the city still needed help with gangs and they wrote in the paper, *The Californian*, that you could call in ideas. There was a new police chief. So I talked to him first and told him how football could help and that these guys want to do something. He thought it was a good idea, but he needed more opinions about it. So I wrote the paper about my idea, and they interviewed me on the phone. An article came out about me starting a "gang football league." That's how it happened.

We had one game that went OK, but we didn't have much support from the city. Then there was this game and there was a lot of shooting. It was a big thing, and it was in the newspaper and they said over twenty shots were fired. Someone got stabbed, but no one was killed. They had to decide afterwards if they would let us continue. I guess they decided it was still a good idea because they let us use the stadium. We had more games on our own and there were no incidents. Then the city council voted to give the league forty thousand dollars. Most of the money goes to hiring police officers to work at the games. The referees get paid, and then there is liability for the stadium. A few of us on the board get small stipends. And we also found some volunteers, but we could use a lot more. One is even a leader of a gang.

The way I get team members is I go out to the streets. I know a lot of people and where they live. First I look at the guys that need help. I don't look only at what the media says, but what's going on in the community with the gang problems. There were big problems between La Posada and Fremont. They're

With one of the teams from the football league

real strong here in Salinas. I got La Posada to play but not Fremont yet. The league isn't going to get them off the streets, but it can show them something. Also I got guys from Castroville to come over here to play. They're mostly Norteño gangs. I chose them because there's always fights with them in Salinas. So if I bring them to play football, they're gonna meet some of the guys here and they'll talk and cooperate. Just by looking at a face and remembering it, that counts a lot. I try to balance the teams between Norteño and Sureño, and one this year will even be mixed. I've learned a lot since the first game.

The idea now is to get the teams out to meet other people and look forward to doing something and not be out on the streets. The guys are about fourteen years old to about twenty-eight. At almost every game we have a short prayer first. I tell them if the referee sees three or more guys fighting at once, their team is going to get penalized. We can't afford shoulder pads or helmets, so I tell them we don't want somebody paralyzed. I tell them to get along and I talk to them about other stuff besides the league. I give them advice, no matter if they listen or not. Usually they appreciate it and thank me after the game. They offer back whatever they can, like respect. I mean they're not going to give me a ring or anything! I tell them that getting along is having a fun game and respecting everyone. Because we're the same, all originally from Mexico.

We need to get that point across. We're all brown; we're all Mexicanos, Chicanos. We all have Mexican pride. Some people have to hear it from other people because they don't understand or never really thought about it. If everyone sat down and took a three-hour class, with a good instructor, there would be a lot of guys that would give more respect to their own race. You know other races, black or white people, they're going to consider us the same, while we're fighting about being Mexicanos and Chicanos. Within our own turf we don't stick together, and that's really stupid.

A lot has changed in the gangs. Like the dress code doesn't really matter anymore. You can't stereotype a gang member, because they can be dressed in nice jeans and shirt and could do a drive-by. There are more girl members, and there are no leaders telling kids what to do and not do. Even kids in elementary school are claiming already, like where I work, at the Boys and Girls Club. It's at the same school I went to, so I relate easier. Two weeks ago, I caught little fifth graders writing gang slogans in the bathroom. I had to tell my supervisor, and they got suspended for a week. I try to tell the kids that gangs are not good, that I was in a gang and I got out, I attend school, and I want to help them. I mean,

With kids at the Boys and Girls Club

look at their age—they're too small, and they should go to school. They're thirteen and under, and their parents should always be involved. They're too young to let them out on the street. I understand the parents may be working in the fields, but I believe it's ridiculous if they are not there for their kids.

I feel very lucky to have my family. I see a future ahead of me now, and it's because of them. I'm at Hartnell College studying to be a probation officer. It's hard to go to school and run the league. It's fun and I love football, but I think it is going to lower some of my grades. But I know it is needed in the community, and it's gonna help me in my future, like for counseling or helping youths in gangs.

I believe the league will help younger kids. It's a time process, not a one-day thing. If they see what the older guys are doing in the league, they are going to be looking at them in a different way. In time, these guys can lecture to kids, be role models, and eventually things will change. The media makes a big deal

Dan at home with his mother, sister, niece, and nephews

out of younger kids in gangs. But crimes are still going to get committed by the older ones, and they're doing the killing.

I know I risk a lot setting up the teams. There could be another shooting. But nobody's willing to do anything. They talk about crime, but they never get active, and just counseling is not gonna help these guys. That's why I don't give up. I'll feel good when it's accomplished. You know, some officials here think these guys are gone and not worth paying attention to. But they're wrong. They don't know them. It's important to always look and pay attention, because everybody's different. If you try to help a person in different ways, on their level, it could be magic. You can get them out.

The Salinas Valley Football League played their last game due to lack of volunteers and community involvement. Dan is now working with Barrios Unidos (Neighborhoods United), a gang intervention program affiliated in several cities. He is also finishing college.

help them to strive
help them to move on
help them to have some future
help them to live long
help them to live life
help them to smile

—from "Feel No Pain," performed by Sade

NINE

How to Help

Often it is one person who will profoundly affect a child's decision to leave a gang. Gang intervention and school programs can help, but kids, like the ones interviewed in this book, often need to replace their trust in the gang with a strong trust in one person. As Saroeum Phoung explains in chapter 2 while talking about Molly Baldwin, director of the program he attended, "I began to put trust on her. It was like being in my gang."

For years, Hewitt Joyner II and Hewitt Joyner III, father and son, have helped kids of many ages and ethnicities leave gangs. A number of methods are effective, they say, and in this chapter they talk about what approaches have worked in the past and what approaches work today. Street life has changed dramatically in the past twenty years, both father and son acknowledge. There is considerably more violence. There are more drugs and broken families. There is more racism and poverty, and for certain groups, such as African-American young men, there are fewer decent-paying jobs. Both agree that the family—and the influence it can have on kids' lives, from street involvement to media violence—is one of the few forces that can counteract the conditions of street life.

Hewitt Reginald Joyner II, fifty-three, was born and raised in the Mission Hill projects in Boston. He started getting into trouble at a young age, he says, because his father was never around. He joined two gangs, but he was able to leave street life with help from mentors at his church. He became a high school state champion in track and field. After graduating from college, he chose to help his community by counseling, teaching, and increasing community support for at-risk youth. He helped create a model recreation program at the Mission Hill projects and worked for the mayor's Youth Activities Commission and on the street with youth gangs. He then moved his family to San Jose, California, where together with his father, he helped develop the first alcohol and drug abuse center for African Americans in Santa Clara County, which helped at-risk and gang-involved youth through a job training program for high school dropouts. He has been employed by the city of San Jose in several capacities working with youth and the elderly. He holds a master's degree in education and also teaches at San Jose State University.

Hewitt Reginald Joyner III, thirty-two, was raised near his father's old neighborhood in Boston until he was eight years old, when his family moved to California. While growing up in San Jose, his exposure to gangs was mostly through his father's work. Eventually he moved his own family back to Boston. Since 1991 he has been employed by Streetworkers, a gang prevention program, part of Boston Community Centers. He works with kids like Patrick and Melissa, profiled in chapters 4 and 7, reaching out to them in schools and on the street. He tries to help children as young as twelve. As he says, he prefers reaching them "before they are hardcore and have a body on them." He also works with trauma victims from gang-related violence at Boston City Hospital and helps run the Peace League, which brings together more than 150 gang members, many from rival gangs, to play basketball.

Hewitt Joyner II and Hewitt Joyner III

Son: When I first moved back to Boston and started working here, what was hard to see was the way kids lived—the

poverty level, the lack of respect, the noncaring attitude, and the lack of love. My work is completely different from Pops's work—because of the murder rate and because the influx of guns is so easy. And back in his day it was cool to be a basketball player. It was cool to sing on the street. The perception of kids now is that it's cool to be a gangster. To carry a 9mm with a full clip in it and have shot someone in the head. It's cool for a nine-year-old to go to school with an AK and just light the whole school up. But the goal is the exact same thing. It's to get into these kids' heads and show them another way, to show them the world that they're living in right now is going to get them in two places—dead or in prison. My goal is to change their lives in any way, for the better.

Father: What you try to do is give kids the knowledge and then try to get them in touch with whatever resource is around. But, it's true that when I was on the street, it wasn't as bad as what Hewie sees. People were poor, but they still cared. There was this one time you could never convince me that a mother didn't care about a child. I don't care how poor they were. It's a biological thing; it wasn't a psychological thing. But when you look at these women today, that are strung out on crack, they don't care about anything but the next hit. And that completely blows my mind.

Son: The reason people do drugs is to escape their lives. If parents had money, they probably wouldn't be doing as many drugs. People need to wake up—it ain't got to do with anything else except for getting people jobs and training them to do a good job and getting them off their butts. And that's also why you have gangs.

Father: But you can't reach a kid unless they are open to listening to what you're going to talk about. You can talk till you're blue in the face. When I was working in schools, I knew that

I had a different rapport with the students. I guess the strength I had is that I was going back to my neighborhood. Every kid in that project knew me. The mothers knew me. You have to gain trust, and I had that already. It makes it so much easier. That's why intervention programs today, rather than bringing in somebody cold, should go into their neighborhoods and find leaders that are already there. Train them, give them a job, and watch the community change. It works. I can't think of any situation where it hasn't. I think what Hewie is doing is just trying to keep these kids alive and start using some logic.

Son: When Pops grew up here, it was different. He knew gang members. But their activity was nothing close to the way these kids act now.

Father: That's right. But the reasons for joining a gang are the same. The outcome is a lot different. These kids today don't have any regard for life, whereas the kids in our day did. You did have some people who were absolutely out of their minds, but nowhere the scale it is now. What hasn't changed today is that kids still look at people who look successful. They've got to have a role model to look at. I'll never forget when I was in a gang, the night Reverend Mike Haynes pulled up on me about two o'clock in the morning, while I was standing up in front of a lounge trying to act like a pimp. He just busted me right out there, saying, "Boy, get off that corner." He was sharp and spoke the best English in the world. He always wanted the best for you, so you could never argue with that.

Son: That's just what I do. If I catch a kid I've been working with out at two o'clock in the morning, I'll tell them not to be out or I'm going to embarrass them in front of their boys. I hate to say this, but I'm going to cuss you out. I'm going to get in your face and make you feel like you're about two inches tall.

Hewitt III discussing his outreach work with kids on the street

In front of all your people, and you will want to go home. But first you try to build a rapport. I try to access that kid and change their lives by any way I can. By all means necessary. Put the kid into a program or into school. If they need some kind of substance training, get them into that. Whatever they need is what you try to get that kid. So I look for kids hanging out with a certain set, with a gang. I don't care what color you are, you're a kid to me. If he's on that block, that kid is down for that minute. If you see that kid constantly with the gang, then they are probably being pulled in. If you see that kid gang-bang, you know that kid is down. Then I introduce myself and I throw out the key points: "Do you have any court cases? Do you need to get back into school? Does your mom or brothers and sisters need any free food?" You can't go out there without something in your pocket. These are kids and they're asking, so I'm gonna give.

Father: Kids know if you're trying to help them. But the way that you're going to really solve the problem now with gangs—and in fact, I'm not even sure you're going to solve it at this point—is to kind of manage it. And for people to share what's successful.

Son: It would be helpful if there was a national link, a coalition of youth workers, violence prevention people, and hospital people that met once or twice a year to share resources and ideas. If it doesn't happen, they'll still have the same crap that's happening in each city. We're all going to be broken apart, and there's going to be duplication of services.

Father: There are successful models out there—which doesn't mean they are going to work in your neighborhood. But essentially if you see something that works, then you have the opportunity to try it. The main goal when I worked with kids on the street was to set up some activities. Isolate the kids. I was trying to get kids that were really rough involved in some activities that were positive. Then as a result of getting them involved with the kinds of things ordinary kids would do—rec center stuff, art, dancing—they could find out who they were. In other words, if kids start thinking that their life is worth something, then they're less likely to go out there and risk it.

Son: One reason kids join gangs is the need for love and support that they're not getting in the household. If they had it at home, they wouldn't need to join the gangs. Kids think there's love on the street, but there's no love. They see gang members hanging out together, giving each other love so they want to be a part of that love. Well, first of all they have to learn how to define love. What is love? Love isn't necessarily just because somebody hangs with you, OK? Love is the person who is going to look out for you.

Father: Well, it's like trying to legislate morality. You can't really teach love. It starts at home. If you don't get it from there, then I don't know where you're going to get it.

Son: If you're not getting it from the house, learn how to love yourself first. You can better yourself. If everything around you is crumbling, then pick yourself out of the rubble. You have to deal with yourself first, because there's not always going to be access to a mentor. Once you pull yourself together, then accessing other people will be easy.

Father: Kids hit the street when they can't find what they need at home. Everything starts with your nucleus. Your home is your nucleus. If that's not an environment that's safe for you, then you're going to go someplace else to find it.

Son: When you see a kid, like the ones I see that are trauma victims, if they are accustomed to violence and death, it becomes the norm. So when they see someone get shot in front of them at age two, they're going to get used to it. By the time they reach fourteen, just think of the way that kid's going to think. And if the kid has no love in his family or he or she thinks that there's no love, death to them is something that they might welcome. Or if they're watching Rambo on TV get shot and put gunpowder in his bullet wound to cure him, then twenty minutes later they think, I can do that and I'll be OK. It's like a Superman complex. You have to control what your kids watch. They should control what is in the newspaper. You do not show a dead person on page one lying in the gutter. You just don't do that. People get used to seeing that, people will act on that.

Father: And what happens is people start glamorizing this violence in order to boost the economy or sell movies and magazines. But I'd go just another step and say neglect has started it, on all kinds of levels—first starting at home. Basically it all goes

Hewitt II believes strongly in his work with kids.

back to parents—how much guidance, how much control. Who's running the house, and is there anybody in charge? It was pretty much the same for me. I remember my dad wasn't there. You've got to take responsibility. So don't have children unless you want children.

Son: And don't have kids unless you're ready. It doesn't take anything to have a baby. But it takes a hell of a lot to be a parent, and you should not have kids unless there is a mother and a father. If you don't feel that you're ready, use a condom. Pops said the main thing. I hate saying "parents" again, 'cause everybody should know it starts with the parents. But a kid does not know how to do one thing right until the parent or someone in that household teaches that kid to do it.

Father: No one trains people to be parents. But if you give kids what they need in terms of who they are and being truthful and open to them as much as you can possibly be, I think you are OK. Also, I think environment is important, and every neighborhood should have the power. When I say power, I mean that people from that community should be able to deal with their own destiny. Because people from that neighborhood are who the kids look up to.

Son: Everything my father did, it's what taught me. I don't think he was trying to teach me, but he did. He is my mentor. I have no others. It is so important that I don't know how to weigh it. I mean, if you don't have a mentor in a young person's life, be it whatever color, the person will grow up to have a lot of problems. Self-esteem will be extremely low. This person will either be a bully or dead.

Father: I guess probably what he picked up was that I think all kids are good kids. They may be misguided. They may be hurting, there may be all kinds of forces working on their psychological makeup, but they're just kids. If you can give them basics, like a little trust, a little love, a sense of stability and confidence, you'd be surprised. Even the worst kids.

Son: I think that's what Pops did. He did a great job. He obviously did, in order to train me to do the job that I do now. But you know, there is no such thing as anybody trying to help and it not taking some effect. If you try, then you're effective.

Father: Well, I guess I was effective, but I could not do what he's doing. All I can say is if people don't now see the need to do whatever they can, then when are they going to? You don't have to go and cure the world; just cure one kid. If you do something with that one kid, he or she may influence another. But don't turn your back.

Son: What would be great is to have a center like the one Pops has told me he wants with all the kids that are court-involved— let's change their lives. Like the kids that are in DYS [Department of Youth Services]. The trade they learn in there is how to seriously gang-bang. So give that kid a trade to learn like bookkeeping or computers, something they like. They'll be a productive member of society.

Father: That is a perfect example of intervention. Give them all a job, something that's marketable. Train them how to do it well and they could grow upon it and would grow within themselves.

Son: Also, all kids like athletics. Any type, I'd say, for all kids and both genders. I don't care if the kid's fat and nasty, they're going to want to try and go shoot a basketball or whatever. And try to keep it fun.

Father: And we could take that same kid and put him through some courses where they learn teamwork, survival, and how to depend on each other. And then they can go home.

Son: So to all these kids and the ones that will read this book, and the ones that are in it: There's mad love out there—just find it. Being a gang member is not the way for you to live your life. And another thing, if you do gang activity, be it just hanging with the group, you *are* down. If you want to get out, you have to get off the block and get away from your boys.

Father: The first thing I would say to these kids is, don't give up hope. You know you've got to believe in yourself. The bottom line is that you are somebody. I mean, it sounds corny, but it's true. You are the future of America. And don't forget it. America goes as you grow.

Signing "Love"

Hope

Hope is a diamond
It never stays the same.
With many sides, many planes.

Hope is the diamond
When your first dream passes by
Don't worry, there's another one to try.

Like the diamond
Hope has endless sides.   —*Valerie Tyson*

"Hope comes from listening to students who share what hope is."   —*Evelyn McLean Brady,*
ninth grade teacher

"Violence is all caused by drugs. Drugs take over everyone, even my mother."   —*Taneka*

"Violence is shakin' my baby because he never sleep, and he had keep screamin' all night, and I'm be so tired, and I know what you mean about violence being inside us, and sometimes I'm so scared of the feelings inside me."   —*Anonymous*

"A mother who cares and protects you when you live on a dangerous street is hope."   —*Natasha White*

"Violence is the police putting telephone books inside me and my homies' jackets so when they hits us with their clubs, the marks don't show."   —*Joe*

"Violence is the bullets coming through the church wall at Xavier's funeral."   —*Shawn*

"Hope is keeping me alive to see my sixteenth birthday."   —*Anonymous*

"Violence is not being able to move to another project even though we told them my family is in danger living here."

—Justin

—Darius Emre

_____

"Hope is a whole day without feeling sorrow."

"What I feel in my heart toward my father for dissin' us is what I think violence is."

—Margaret

_____

"Hope is when I feel loved by my mom."

—Marisa Salgado

"Violence is being at a party and suddenly everybody's screamin' and the glass had sprayed all over, my boyfriend's cousin had yelled he hit, and everybody's running out the back door and it's five degrees out, and you don't even feel the cold."

—Lakeisha

_____

"Hope comes when everything else goes."

—Antonio Wiggins

_____

"Hope is the essence that keeps you looking forward to life. Some people hope for money. Some people hope for life's basic necessities. But hope no one can buy, sell or take away from you. Hope is your inner fire. It is the determination that keeps you going, and not give up. With one spark, the hope you share can give others the light of hope for themselves."

—Keri Messimi

_____

From a written unit on surviving violence with hope, supervised by Evelyn Brady at Riverside High School, Buffalo, New York

Getting Help

If you're in a gang and you want to get out, if you are thinking of joining one, or if you have a friend or brother or sister you are concerned about, here are some suggestions about how to get help.

Choosing someone to talk with about your feelings, thoughts, or questions is a good first step.

Find someone you are comfortable with or someone you look up to. It is probably best if that person is not in a gang, unless he or she is supportive about helping you get out or stay out. If the person *is* in a gang, be sure he or she is someone you trust and someone who will keep what you tell him or her private. If you are currently in a gang, having word get out to the wrong people could be dangerous, so be careful about whom you speak with.

Talk with someone in your family first, if you can.

If you feel you can't talk with your own parents, consider talking with a friend's parents.

Try talking with your teachers.

Your school may have some helpful resources and services:

If your school has a counseling program, talk with a counselor.

If your school does not have counseling on campus, ask if they can refer you to someplace that does.

Find out if your school has conflict resolution groups or any kind of gang prevention or support groups. If a program is available, check it out.

Your community may also offer some programs that could be helpful. Here are some ideas about how to find them:

Go to your local place of worship and speak with a priest, pastor, or rabbi. The church or synagogue may have after-school programs, counseling, or other help for gang kids.

Call up the local Boys and Girls Club or your YMCA and ask them about their programs. They are usually listed in the phone book under the city or town's name.

Look in the white pages under "community services" or under your community's name. Call the organizations listed and ask about their programs.

Look up teen or youth agencies or hot lines in the phone book.

Call any adult organization that you know of that might help kids, such as the Rotary Club or Big Brothers and Sisters of America.

Call your local police station to see if they have referrals for gang programs or have a gang task force. Then ask them to connect you to that section.

Look in your local paper for articles about programs that help gang members or children and teens who are having problems.

Does your community have any special sports clubs or groups for kids or specifically for gang members? If so, sign up and check them out.

Sign up for an after-school program, and find someone there to talk to.

If you decide to participate in any of these programs, it's smart to tell your parents or a family member first, so they know where you are.

Most important, find *someone* to help you.

Intervention Programs

For a booklet listing gang intervention programs in your area and nationwide, call (toll-free) **1-888-GANGS NO**, *or ask your parents or a teacher to call for you. The following is a listing of some of the programs and schools mentioned in this book.*

Bruce Wall Ministries
Gangs Anonymous
Bruce Wall, director
Dorchester Temple Baptist Church
670 Washington Street
Dorchester, Massachusetts 02124
(617) 282-7794
Bruce Wall and Craig McMullen, copastors

> With programs such as after-school tutoring, Gangs Anonymous, and parenting classes, as well as weekly Christian services, Bruce Wall Ministries helps children, teens, and parents find assistance in dealing with many problems, including those related to violence and gangs. Committed to the community, this church and its many services bring children and their families closer.

Gardner Community Teen Center
City of San Jose Teen Centers
520 W. Virginia Street
San Jose, California 95125
(408) 277-2761
Tony Torres, youth program coordinator

> A teen center providing social, recreational, and educational programs. Programs include boxing, baseball, and Aztec dancing. By providing youths with a place to go and something to do, this teen center helps eliminate neighborhood problems such as drugs, crime, and gang activity.

Little Havana Institute
300 S.W. 12th Avenue
Miami, Florida 33130
(954) 649-2952
Martha Young, principal

An alternative education program run by the Cuban American National Council in connection with Dade County Public Schools for at-risk students in grades seven through eleven. Little Havana helps kids who did not succeed in traditional schools because of truancy, home problems, limited English proficiency, or other obstacles. The program provides a family atmosphere and encourages good relationships among students and between students and teachers. On- and off-campus counseling is offered for at-risk kids, including those in gangs. This school encourages team projects, peer tutoring, and learning in a cooperative setting.

ROCA
148 Washington Avenue
Chelsea, Massachusetts 02150
(617) 889-5210
Molly Baldwin, director

ROCA (the name means "rock" in Spanish) is a multicultural youth development program for kids and their parents addressing youth and health issues. It provides art, recreational, health, educational, and vocational programs and uses street outreach, leadership principles, and community organizing to ensure its effectiveness. It runs on principles defined by young people, such as safety, mentoring, creativity, love, peace, and justice. Part of ROCA's philosophy is the belief that youths are a strong resource for solving their communities' most urgent problems, such as gangs; ROCA is also founded on the belief that kids are basically good, and when supported and challenged properly, they choose to be responsible, productive, and active members of these communities.

The Starting Place
2057 Coolidge Street
Hollywood, Florida 33020
(954) 925-2225
Sheldon Shaffer, director
Tammy Tucker, clinical director

> A nonprofit residential and outpatient facility for treatment of youths and adults with substance abuse problems. Youths thirteen to seventeen years old are accepted for the residential program, which includes on-site teachers. An early intervention program helps educate kids and families about how to deal with a range of problems from drug abuse to gang involvement. Individual, group, and family therapy focuses on developing skills in anger management and communication.

Streetworkers
Boston Community Centers
1010 Massachusetts Avenue
Boston, Massachusetts
(617) 635-4920 ext. 2214
Hewitt R. Joyner III, program manager

> Working in schools and on the street, this program gives youths and their families access to health and social services, as well as to educational, recreational, and intervention services, many of which focus on gang involvement or drug and alcohol abuse. Streetworkers also help kids and their families with vocational planning and assist with conflicts between students and between students and school administrators.

Glossary

AK: a brand of automatic weapon, such as an AK-47

Angka: literally "a Communist government," implying dictatorship or martial law; used by the Khmer Rouge to refer to themselves

basehead: a cocaine addict who freebases

Blood: a member of the Bloods, a type of gang that has spread all over the United States and is now made up of various ethnicities and has many offshoots. The rival gang is usually a Crip gang.

blue: a color various gangs use to claim their affiliation

body on, as in **to have a body on you**: to have committed a murder

booting or **booting up**: shooting up heroin

Brown Pride: a Chicano gang; usually separate from Norteño or Sureño gangs

bucking: shooting at

Chicanismo: identification with and pride in being Chicano

Chicano: Mexican American; usually used to refer to those who identify with and are proud of their Mexican heritage

cholo/chola: a kid from a barrio, or Latino/Hispanic neighborhood; can refer to a gang member; can have a negative connotation. *Cholo* is the masculine form, *chola* the feminine.

claiming: acknowledging or stating that one belongs to a gang

crack: a highly addictive, smokable form of crystallized cocaine

crew: group or gang

Crip: a member of the Crips, a prolific gang that exists in many locations throughout the United States and is now made up of various ethnicities and has many offshoots. The rival gang is usually a Blood gang.

diesel: heroin

down, as in **down for your gang**: suggests being heavily involved in one's gang and being willing to do anything for fellow members, supporting them 100 percent

drive-by: a shooting committed from a moving vehicle, usually involving multiple gunshots from an automatic weapon

DSS: Department of Social Services, the Massachusetts state agency that is responsible for the care and protection of abused and neglected children and that provides an array of services for children and families

DYS: Department of Youth Services, the Massachusetts state agency responsible for providing care and services for crime-involved teens and other youths

ése: Spanish term meaning "guy" or "you," as in "Hey, *ése*"; used by Latino/Hispanic street youths

Folk Nation: a relatively newly formed gang, usually multiethnic, existing in various locations in the United States

forty: a forty-ounce can of beer

gang-bang: to be involved in gang activities, often violent, criminal activities

GED: General Equivalency Diploma, equivalent to a high school degree

H: heroin

homeboy, homegirl, homie: someone from one's neighborhood or gang

Khmer: means "people" in the Cambodian language; refers to ethnic Cambodians

Khmer Rouge: literally "Red People" or "Reds"; a Communist guerrilla force that waged war against the Cambodian government, toppling it in 1975. Under Pol Pot, it then undertook a ruthless collectivization campaign, in which three million people died. It was ousted in 1979 but continues to field an army and pose a threat.

Kmai or Khmer: the language of the Cambodian people

Latin Queens: a female counterpart to Latin Kings, a Latino-based gang

loco: "crazy" in Spanish; frequently used in gang names, such as Madeira Barrio Locos

Mad Dog: an inexpensive, potent brand of alcoholic beverage

narcs: narcotics agents

Norteño: Spanish word for "northerner"; a Mexican-American gang whose members have lived in the United States a long time or were born here. Can also be used to refer to a gang based in northern California. Also called a fourteener gang, referring to the fourteenth letter of the alphabet, *N*, standing for *north*.

OG: original or veteran gang member. OG's are usually older, have reputations as gang members, and are looked to for advice.

poghma: Khmer word for "good friend"

quinceñera: a celebration or coming-out party for fifteen-year-old Latino/Hispanic girls

red: a color various gangs use to claim their affiliation

set: the group in a neighborhood that is affiliated with a main gang

shot callers: older gang members who act as leaders, make the rules, and "call the shots"

sign: to show one's gang sign, a hand gesture unique to the gang

skinhead: a member of a gang that usually espouses white supremacist beliefs

streetworker: a youth outreach worker

Sureño: Spanish word for "southerner"; a Mexican-American gang whose members are recent immigrants to the United States or were born in Mexico. Can also be used to refer to a gang based in southern California. Also called thirteener gangs, referring to the thirteenth letter of the alphabet, *M*, standing for *Mexico*.

tag or **tag up**: to draw or paint gang signs such as in murals or graffiti, usually to protect or label turf

trip: to take psychedelic drugs, such as LSD

vago: Spanish word for "vagrant"; sometimes used in Latino/Hispanic gang names

veteranos: Spanish word for "veterans"; used to refer to veteran gang members

violated: beaten up or killed in retaliation for breaching trust with or leaving a gang

wannabe: used to refer to someone who wants to be in a gang

weed: one of the many terms used for marijuana

Initiation Terms

beaten in: initiated into a gang by being beaten up. Also referred to as being jumped in or walked in. Being walked in involves walking down a line of gang members, each of whom can beat the newcomer.

blessed in: automatically allowed to join a gang because a family member is already a member or because one has previously proven oneself worthy. Also called to slide in.

sexed in: initiated into a gang by having sex with one or more gang members. Also called being trained in.

Recommended Further Reading

Bing, Leon. *Do or Die*. New York: HarperCollins, 1991.

California Department of Education. *On Alert! Gang Prevention: School In-service Guidelines*. Sacramento: California Department of Education, 1994.

California Department of Justice. *Gangs: A Statewide Directory of Programs*. Sacramento: Office of the Attorney General, California Department of Justice, 1994.

California Legislature, Joint Committee on Organized Crime and Gang Violence. *Alternatives to Street Gangs: Urban Services Restoration Corps and Neighborhood Academies*. Sacramento: Joint Publications, 1989.

Canada, Geoffrey. *Fist Stick Knife Gun: A Personal History of Violence in America*. Boston: Beacon, 1995.

Conly, Catherine H. *Street Gangs: Current Knowledge and Strategies*. Issues and Practices in Criminal Justice series. Washington, D.C.: National Institute of Justice, 1993.

Cummings, Scott, and Daniel J. Monti, editors. *Gangs: The Origins and Impact of Contemporary Youth Gangs in the U.S.* Albany: State University of New York Press, 1993.

DeJong, William, Ph.D. *Preventing Interpersonal Violence Among Youth: An Introduction to School, Community, and Mass Media Strategies*. Washington, D.C.: National Institute of Justice, 1994.

Ewing, Charles Patrick. *When Children Kill: The Dynamics of Juvenile Homicide*. Lexington, Kentucky: Lexington Books, 1990.

Fremon, Celeste. *Father Greg and the Homeboys: The Extraordinary Journey of Father Greg Boyle and His Work with the Latino Gangs of East L.A.* New York: Hyperion, 1995.

Hanson, Kitty. *Rebels in the Streets: The Story of New York's Girl Gangs*. Englewood Cliffs, N.J.: Prentice-Hall, 1964.

Harris, Mary G. *Cholas: Latino Girls and Gangs*. New York: AMS Press, 1988.

Hernandez, Arturo. *Peace in the Streets*. Salt Lake City: Northwest Publishing, 1995.

Hinojosa, Maria. *CREWS: Gang Members Talk to Maria Hinojosa*. New York: Harcourt Brace, 1995.

Huff, Ronald C., editor. *Gangs in America*. Thousand Oaks, Calif.: Sage Publications, 1990.

Jankowski, Martín Sánchez. *Islands in the Street: Gangs and American Urban Society*. Berkeley: University of California Press, 1991.

Kline, Malcolm W. *Street Gangs and Street Workers*. Englewood Cliffs, N.J.: Prentice-Hall, 1971.

Kotlowitz, Alex. *There Are No Children Here: The Story of Two Boys Growing Up in the Other America*. New York: Doubleday, 1991.

Kozol, Jonathan. *Savage Inequalities: Children in America's Schools*. New York: Crown, 1991.

Minow, Newton N., and Craig L. Lamay. *Abandoned in the Wasteland: Children, Television and the First Amendment*. New York: Hill & Wang, 1995.

Monti, Daniel S. *Wannabe: Gangs in Suburbs and Schools*. Oxford: Cambridge USA–Blackwell, 1994.

Moore, Joan W. *Going Down to the Barrio: Homeboys and Homegirls in Change*. Philadelphia: Temple University Press, 1991.

Murray, James. *Fifty Things You Can Do about Guns*. Highland Park, N.J.: RD Publishing, 1994.

Ngor, Haing, with Roger Warner. *Cambodian Odyssey*. New York: Warner, 1989.

Nightingale, Carl Husemoller. *On the Edge: A History of Poor Black Children and Their American Dreams*. New York: Basic Books, 1993.

Previte, Mary Taylor. *Hungry Ghosts: One Woman's Mission to Save America's Empty Souls*. Grand Rapids, Mich.: Zondervan, 1993.

Prothrow-Stith, Deborah, and Michaele Weissman. *Deadly Consequences: How Violence Is Destroying Our Teenage Population and a Plan to Begin Solving the Problems*. New York: HarperCollins, 1991.

Riis, Jacob A. *How the Other Half Lives: Studies Among the Tenements of New York*. New York: Sagamore, 1957.

Rodriguez, J. Luis. *Always Running: La Vida Loca, Gang Days in L.A.* New York: Curbstone, 1993.

Skolnick, Jerome H. *Gang Organization and Migration: Drugs, Gangs and Law Enforcement*. Sacramento: Office of the Attorney General, California Department of Justice, 1990.

Spergel, Irving A., Ronald L. Chance, and David G. Curry. *National Youth Gang Suppression and Intervention Program*. Juvenile Justice Bulletin series. U.S. Department of Justice, Office of Juvenile Justice and Delinquency Prevention, Washington D.C.: 1991.

Taylor, Carl S. *Girls, Gangs, Women and Drugs*. East Lansing: Michigan State University Press, 1993.

Thrasher, Frederic Milton. *The Gang: A Study of 1,313 Gangs in Chicago*. Chicago: University of Chicago Press, 1963.

Vigil, James Diego. *Barrio Gangs: Street Life and Identity in Southern California*. Austin: University of Texas Press, 1988.

Watts, Tim J. *The New Gangs: Young, Armed, and Dangerous*. Monticello, N.Y.: Vance Bibliographies, 1988.

Wilson, James Q. *Thinking About Crime*. New York: Basic Books, 1975.

FOR YOUNGER READERS

Barden, Renardo. *Gangs*. New York: Crestwood House, 1989.

Clise, Michelle Durson. *Stop the Violence Please*. Seattle: University of Washington Press, 1994.

Gardner, Sandra. *Street Gangs in America*. New York: Franklin Watts, 1992.

Goodwillie, Susan, editor. *Voices from the Future: Our Children Tell Us About Violence in America*. New York: Children's Express Press, 1993.

Greenberg, Keith Elliot. *Out of the Gang*. Minneapolis: Lerner Publications, 1992.

McCall, Nathan. *Makes Me Wanna Holler: A Young Black Man in America*. New York: Random House, 1994.

Miller, Mary Ann. *Coping with Weapons and Violence in Your School and on Your Streets*. New York: Rosen Publishing Group, 1993.

Mowry, Jess. *Way Past Cool*. New York: Farrar, Straus & Giroux, 1992.

Myers, Walter Dean. *Scorpions*. New York: HarperCollins, 1988.

Osman, Karen. *Gangs*. San Diego: Lucent, 1992.

Thomas, Anika. *Life in the Ghetto*. Kansas City: Landmark Editions, 1991.

Webb, Margot. *Coping with Street Gangs*. New York: Rosen Publishing Group, 1990.

Acknowledgments

First I would like to thank everyone who is interviewed and photographed in this book, along with their families. Obviously, without them, the book would not exist, nor would I have had the many new experiences they gave me. Also, I could not have worked in San Jose and Boston without the help of Hewitt Joyner II and Hewitt Joyner III.

This book could not have been produced without: Ann Rider, my editor, who stayed on top of my whereabouts and my never-ending research and was continually encouraging, and my agent, Sarah Winer, at William Morris, who was helpful and patient, maintained a sense of humor, and was also a good friend. Many thanks as well to John Keller for working on this book with professionalism, patience, and enthusiasm. And thanks to Gina Hagen and Hannah Mahoney for their expertise and for all the extra time and energy they put in.

My friends have been exceptionally supportive, tolerating my constantly changing addresses and plans because of this work. They opened their homes to me, shipped me equipment, sent me articles, and took care of my cat, home, and office. I am grateful for their patience, care, and constant friendship.

Many people helped make this intensely rewarding but difficult project possible. I feel very fortunate to have had them around me—the many people of all ages and professions who referred me to these youths and their families, as well as everyone I worked with and stayed with along the way. Because I was working in so many locations for several years, I am bound to miss recognizing someone who lent me an important hand. I hope I have already expressed my appreciation to everyone for the generous and open manner in which they helped me. I would like in particular to say thank you to:

California: Boys & Girls Club of Salinas; Vercila Chaçon: County of Santa Clara Social Services Agency; Tyrone Cheng; Camden Youth Center; Enrique Degregori; Tony Torres, Rudy Martinez, and the staff of the Gardner Community Teen Center; Kristen Hunter; José Ortiz; Amy Pofcher; Claire Schwartz; Patrick and Helaine Tregenza; and Gil Villagran, Nuestra Casa Youth Center.

Massachusetts: Tracy Lithcutt, Boston Community Centers; Barbara Greenberg; Sally Kolodkin; Joe Zwicker and Diane McGlaughlin, Massachusetts Correctional Legal Services; the staff of ROCA; Bruce Wall Ministries and Gangs Anonymous staff; Dorchester Baptist Temple Church; John Dunham, Craig McMullen, and Karen Wall; Suzanne Kreiter and Paul Drake, *Boston Globe*; Julie Schecter; Will Hapgood; Nan Wetherhorn; and Martinol Chan, Cambodian Community Center.

Florida: Robin Burns; Bradley Collins; Judge Robert Collins, Chief Juvenile Judge, Broward County; Xavier Cortada, Casey Initiative; Victor Diaz, Esq.; Glamour Shots; Akilah Touré and Margaret Zehren, Legal Services of Greater Miami; José Szapocznik, director, Center for Family Studies, University of Miami School of Medicine; John Walsh and James Walsh, Child Welfare Legal Services, State of Florida Department of Health and Rehabilitative Services; the P.A.C.E. Center for Girls; Barbara Wade, Positive, Inc.; Wilson Palacias; Charles Radice; Marion Kiley and José Marcalle, Regis House; Martha and Aaron Schecter; Sheldon Shaffer, Tammy Tucker, Suzanne Leitner, Sheila Wenck, Sylvia Poro, Jackie Calloway, and the residential staff at The Starting Place.

In addition, I would like to thank those who helped me locate and translate excellent and moving poetry and writing: Jennie Atkinson, Boys and Girls Club of Charlestown; Evelyn Brady, Riverside High School; Ondina Duarte; Linda Hannon, Department of Youth Services, Westboro Secure Treatment Center; Jim Hight, United Youth; Diane Scott, City Year, Boston; OK Socheat, Mission of Cambodia to the United Nations. And I'm grateful to all the kids who submitted their writing, whether or not it appears in this book.

Many thanks as well to Alex Kotlowitz for agreeing to write the foreword.

And I would like to give special thanks for housing; excellent research, photography, and transcription assistance; darkroom use; transportation; and in general great care and support to: Julie Allison; Molly Baldwin; Lois and Fred Feinstein; Alison Forker; Hank and Estelle Lowenstein; Yolanda Mancilla, Ph.D., Center for Family Studies, University of Miami School of Medicine; Donna Shank; Diane Van de Mark, M.D.; Regina Moran; Bruce Wall; Martha Young; and to my grandmother, Esther Shustick, to my brothers, and to my mother and father, who helped sustain me in many ways throughout this project.

*For a booklet listing gang intervention programs in your area and nationwide,
call (toll-free) 1-888-GANGS NO.*